heaven's
kitchen
devotional

alexis vazquez
cover art by morgan harper nichols

HEAVEN'S KITCHEN

Published on: October 16, 2019

Interior design by: Clara Stone of Reader Central

Cover Art by: Morgan Harper Nichols

Edited by: Adele Brinkley

Location used for Promotional Materials: Fallen Oak Farms, Valrico, Florida

Photographer for author bio pic: Richard Toussaint

Dedicated to the incredible guy who makes me his wife someday. I'll be waiting for the day God brings us together. I'll be waiting to share endless meals at our kitchen table. I'll be waiting to celebrate the unmatched man of God I know you'll be. There will be no comparison to you, my love. And when God gives you victory, I'll always throw you the after party. Here's to all that God is preparing in the kitchens of heaven for us.

week 1

PREP WORK

Mise En Place

*"Because of your little faith," He told them. "For I assure you:
If you have faith the size of a mustard seed, you will tell this
mountain, 'move from here to there,' and it will move.
Nothing will be impossible for you.
Matthew 17:20 HCSB*

There's a cooking term called *mise en place* which is French for "setting in place." It's one of the key techniques professional chefs live by and it is known as a basic culinary skill. It looks like having all your ingredients and tools ready to go before you start cooking. You may be thinking, "What's the big deal? I can just grab things as I go." but the process of preparing and cooking a meal moves rather quickly in a kitchen. You avoid forgetting ingredients and steps in the recipe by preparing everything in advance. The concept of *mise en place* may appear time-consuming at first, but it ends up saving the chef time and stress at the end, when the meal is cooked to perfection and ready to be served. The reason I am explaining a French cooking term to you is because I want to demonstrate that God is perfect at setting the chapters of our stories in place. He is not wasting His time or ours. He set the seasons in place so that there would be a time to sow and a time to reap. He set the moon and sun in the sky, so we would never have to walk in the dark. And He's setting divine pieces of our stories in place for us too.

I originally planned to write this devotional centered around waiting when it came to singleness. But the more I looked around, the more I realized that everyone is waiting for something: a career breakthrough, a positive pregnancy test, financial provision, a prodigal child to come back home, or the love of your life to come to sweep you off your feet. Whatever it is that we are waiting for, the waiting room is full of questions, and while we are asking them, God is inviting us to join Him in a different setting with a different perspective.

He yearns to push us gently out of that cold, dark waiting room full of questions and wondering and toward a table- a table prepared just for you and me. And at this table, people are gathered. It's you, it's me, waiting, anticipating, hoping. It's right outside His kitchen. In fact, it's so close to His kitchen that you can hear Him speaking to you while He's in there cooking. We can smell the fragrance of something good being prepared even though we can't quite put our noses on what it is yet.

That fragrance stirs up our hope. We can see and hear the stories unfolding around us as we gather around this table. These stories being shared are letting us know that we are not alone. Time after time, God may bring a few appetizers out, not to tease us, but to set us up for what's coming next. It's important to note that our God is kind. It can be so easy to believe the lie that He is not when we feel like He's keeping something from us. If we could only grasp the simple fact that He is waiting for us, maybe then, we would extend a little more grace to Him when He seems to be taking a little too long in Heaven's Kitchen. He longs for us to come and join Him at His table. He knows that sitting at His table doesn't make waiting easier for us, but He also knows what we don't. He knows what He's preparing and how to prepare it. He knows that if we could only peek inside His kitchen, we would be overjoyed with excitement, or overwhelmed because we wouldn't be quite sure how all the ingredients fit yet. Peeking inside would take away what makes our relationship with God so special, trust. You can't have a good relationship without it. If we knew it all, what would we need Him for? What would our dialogue with God sound like if there were no questions?

The mystery of God is what makes our journey a quest of faith through which He prepares us for what we're preparing for. Faith is the first ingredient in our relationship with God. Faith is the foundation for any great recipe in God's kitchen. He can't do much without it, but with a little bit of faith, even if it is the size of a mustard seed, He will cook up miracles we would have never been able to prepare ourselves.

wow this is so good

TABLE TALK

---

2 Corinthians 2:15 tells us that we are the fragrance of Christ. One way we can tell that a meal is going to be good is by the aroma it carries throughout the room and if we're around it for too long, we start to smell like it! It's not that great in a literal sense, but it poses these questions: Am I spending enough time around Jesus that I smell like Him? Can people recognize Him when they are around me? Is

my lack of faith coming from a lack of drawing near to God at His table? I challenge you to draw near to Him throughout this devotional. Don't just read my words, read the Scriptures for yourself and see how He speaks directly to your heart in your season of waiting.

- continue to be intentional about the time with God
- He wants us close to Him

day 2

Can God Spread A Table In The Wilderness?

Psalm 78:1-39

Tucked in the psalms is a song that isn't blatantly about waiting. Psalm 78 is not only a psalm but also a *maskil*, meaning its intention is not only to praise God but to impart wisdom. Asaph, the writer, starts the psalm by getting people's attention. He's basically saying, "Hey! Listen up! Tell it to your kids, your grandkids, their kids, and everybody else- God is faithful. These are the marvelous things He's done." (author's paraphrase) He encourages the people of God to not forget the wonderful works God has performed. He calls us out for having short-term memory. And when I say "us," I mean, the children of God.

Although according to the scriptures, Asaph is speaking to an audience of Israelites, are we really that much different than they? We are set apart by God as His children. We call Him Lord, but do we really trust Him with our lives?

Let's take a closer look at the Israelites and their faith according to Asaph's psalm. He says in verse 9, "The Ephraimite archers turned back on the day of battle." These people had what they needed to carry out a battle, but they still didn't trust God to win it for them. The Israelites literally saw God part a sea for them, lead them by a cloud, bring water out of a rock, and they *still* doubted Him. As the Psalm says, "They spoke against God, saying, 'Can God spread a table in the wilderness? He struck the rock so that the water gushed out and streams overflowed. Can he also give bread or provide meat for his people?'" (Psalm 78:19-20) They were so busy looking at what they were still missing that they missed the miracle of what He had already given them.

Do we have faith that God can prepare a table in the wilderness for us, especially, when we've already seen Him do it before? The beauty of Psalm 78 is that even in the Israelites' doubt and complaining, God had mercy on them. His love was (and still is) unconditional, and He continued to give them a taste of His goodness, hoping they'd finally grasp His unending faithfulness.

Yet he was compassionate; He atoned for their guilt and did not destroy them. He often turned His anger aside and did not unleash all his wrath. He remembered that they were only flesh. Psalm 78:38-39

God is on our side even when we are too busy with our own selfish desires to be on His side. He remembers that we are only flesh. In the middle of our barren wilderness, will we remember the God who's done wonderful things for us?

TABLE TALK

What does your current wilderness look like? In what ways has God rained down manna from heaven for you in the midst of it? Can you relate to the Israelites who quickly forgot God's faithfulness in the desert? *sometimes get too busy*

Olive trees flourish in desert climates. They tolerate drought well because of their sturdy root system. They can live for centuries if pruned regularly. In biblical times, the oil produced from the trees was used for cooking, anointing, and illuminating a room. Psalm 52:8 says to us, "But I am like an olive tree flourishing in the house of God; I trust in God's unfailing love forever and ever."

Can we challenge ourselves to be more like olive trees, who flourish, not only in God's house but also in whatever dry place we find ourselves? In the wilderness, we still possess purpose, we can still bless people, and we can still provide light- just like an olive tree.

Sometimes Seasons of Preparation
Look A Lot Like Shepherding Sheep

1 Samuel 24:5-7, 1 Samuel 16:1, Psalm 78:70-72

At the end of Psalm 78, Asaph writes of King David, whom God chose over all His rebellious children. God took him from shepherding sheep to shepherding people. To be honest, I am not quite sure why the psalmist ends the second-longest psalm in the Bible with a highlight on King David. Perhaps, David was no stranger to waiting on God.

David was anointed to be king at a young age, but he didn't become king right then and there. Bible scholars estimate 15-22 years lapsed between the time David was anointed to be king and the time he actually became king. Not even slaying a giant with a rock expedited the process for him. Regardless of the timetable, God had been preparing him to become the greatest King Israel had ever seen, even when it didn't seem like he'd ever trade in his shepherd's staff for a crown.

David even put up with King Saul wanting to kill him (1 Samuel 19). Saul grew to hate him, but David kept trusting in God's plan. He had the opportunity to kill Saul in 1 Samuel 24, but his heart remained steadfast on the Lord. He said, "The Lord forbid that I should do such a thing to my master, the Lord's anointed, or lay my hand on him; for he is the anointed of the Lord" (1 Samuel 24:6). David knew God had appointed Saul to be king in that season, and even though he knew he was anointed to become king someday, he chose to continue to wait and honor God and His plan.

When I think about all the dreams God has placed on my heart, shepherding sheep as David did, is not a part of my vision. However, it is a part of the big picture. Sheep tend to go astray, and shepherds need to protect and care for them at all hours of the day. I'm sure the smell wasn't that great for David either. But what if shepherding sheep was God's way of growing a heart of patience within him? What if tending to sheep is what prepared him to shepherd an entire nation? Our waiting seasons may be filled with tedious work and even enemies who are trying to attack us on all sides, but they are never wasted seasons.

TABLE TALK

To understand better what made David a great king, we must look at the king who came before him, Saul. Saul's insecurities and lack of trust in God led to his fall. Read 1 Samuel 13:7-14. Unlike David, Saul was impatient and took matters into his own hands when Samuel clearly told him to wait on him (1 Samuel 10:8). Surrounded by his enemies, Saul became anxious when Samuel didn't show up to offer the sacrifice before going to war.

What was David's reaction in the presence of his enemies? (See Psalm 23:5) Like Saul, have you ever put a "but" when God said, "just wait"? Samuel showed up right after Saul took matters into his own hands. Sometimes, deliverance is closer than we think, but we have to choose to keep trusting God even when we feel like He's running late. How did Saul's lack of trust and impatience impact his future?

day 4

While You Are Sleeping, God Is Working

Exodus 16, Matthew 11:28-30

There is nothing quite like waking up to the smell of breakfast being made in the kitchen, especially when it's bacon. Am I right? It's hard to get me out of bed in the morning, but if you tell me breakfast is ready, you will see me become a morning person really quickly.

True story. I am sure the same is true for most people unless you don't like breakfast, and in that case, you need an extra dose of Jesus in your life. The Israelites were well acquainted with God making breakfast for them. He made breakfast for them for 40 years in the wilderness. In Psalm 78, Asaph reminded the Israelites of God's provision when He rained bread down from Heaven. Exodus 16 describes the whole story in greater detail.

The Israelites were grumbling and complaining in the desert. They were hungry and desperate. It sounds a lot like me whenever I am waiting for God to do something. They even went as far as to say that they were better off in Egypt! (Exodus 16:3) Their hunger and desperation clouded their perception to the point where they would have rather stayed enslaved than set free. I, myself, am guilty of this toxic mentality. I look at whatever my season of waiting is, and I think to myself, "Well if I just would have stayed where I was. I wouldn't be in this uncomfortable place right now."

Every season of waiting I have sat in has been a direct result of me being obedient to each step God has asked me to take. It's part of the preparation process for wherever He's leading us to next, and as long as we're on this side of heaven, He will always be leading us upward and onward. The beautiful thing is, even in our grumbling, God is so gracious. When God heard the complaints of His children in the wilderness, He said to them, "At twilight, you shall eat meat, and in the morning, you shall be filled with bread" (Exodus 16:12) He had them go to sleep and when they arose in the morning, bread was encompassing the ground. While they were sleeping, He was working. Morning by morning, they gathered the bread from heaven (Exodus 16:21).

Now, even in the miracle of God raining down bread from heaven, some still struggled with a stubborn spirit. It was hard for some of them to trust that God would continue to provide what He promised. God had commanded that they collect a double portion of bread on the sixth day, so they would have enough bread for the Sabbath, but some still went looking for bread on the seventh day. In the same way, our stubbornness can kill the trust that God is trying to birth in us.

Moses grew frustrated with them for not keeping God's commandments and ordered them to stay home and rest. How many times has God told us to rest? How many times will He need to tell us to be still? He's so full of mercy that he will tell us as many times as we need to hear it, that's for sure.

One thing I am trying to repeat to myself in my season of waiting is that God has already worked out what I am worried about. I don't need to go looking to fill my hunger when he has already provided my double portion. I need to go home and rest. While we are sleeping, He is working. While we are sleeping, He is preparing. While we are sleeping and dreaming of a new season, He graciously hears the grumbling cries and the hunger pains of our hearts and gives us just what we need and how much we need of it (Exodus 16:17). While we are sleeping, I can imagine, He is smiling. He knows the story ends with a promise fulfilled.

TABLE TALK

God's day literally starts at night. Have you ever realized that? Every day starts at midnight. What are some things you are praying God is working on as you sleep? If you struggle with being still, ask God to give you a heart to rest when you are tempted to figure out His plans and purposes on your own. God's Word promises in Psalm 121 that He neither slumbers nor sleeps. We all experience the exhaustion that comes from waiting on the Lord. We get so tired we can barely spit out words to pray. It's okay to be worn out as long as we're falling into the arms of a loving Father who never tires of delighting in every detail of our lives.

future husband, break through for parents
future home,

What God Is Preparing You For Is Much Greater Than What You Have Prepared For

Luke 23:55-56, Luke 24:1-9, Mark 9:31

I think one of the hardest parts about waiting is the constant pity party we are tempted to throw for ourselves. "Well, this is pointless. Why am I even praying? Why am I even trying? What's the point? I do not feel like praying today. I think I'll just stay in bed and binge watch a mindless show on Netflix all day. [insert sigh here]" Maybe it's just me, but I have invited myself to a fair share of pity parties. I might as well pick up some balloons and invite people to join me. That's how bad my frustration gets sometimes. I become so hopeless, it creates a veil of deception over my eyes that causes me to believe the lie that God is not faithful. And when I stop believing God is faithful, I can't find the strength to continue seeking Him in my waiting.

In Luke 23, Mary Magdalene, Mary, and Salome, (another one of Jesus' disciples) had prepared spices to go anoint Jesus in the tomb. They had gone to the tomb in the early dawn as the sun was rising. They had no idea that they were not going to anoint the body of Jesus, but rather find that He was alive and had fulfilled what He had promised. He had been crucified, but He rose on the third day just like He said He would. I can only assume that as the women were walking to the tomb that early morning, they were somber and maybe feeling hopeless.

What were they supposed to do now? Their teacher, their friend, their Savior, was gone. How could the story get better from here? He was dead. There was no coming back from that, right? They were probably filled with questions, wondering what God would do next. To their surprise, they were walking directly into what God would do next. The tomb was empty! A promise fulfilled, and they were the first ones to witness it. We read yesterday about God working while we are sleeping, so I think it's no coincidence that this promise came at early dawn. In Mark's account, it says the women went to the tomb at the rising of the sun. The beautiful thing is that these women woke up early in all their pain and disappointment. They had a task. They were going to anoint the body of Jesus.

You and I both know that God works while we are sleeping. Sleeping while God works doesn't give us answers to the longings in our hearts, but it gives us the rest we need to do what God has called us to do in the process. What if we took the posture of these women? I am sure that waking up early to anoint Jesus' body brought hurt and questions about their future, but they got up anyway. They did what honored God anyway. Despite what we are feeling, despite the unknowns, what if we got up and served God anyway? Perhaps by getting some sleep, waking up, and doing what we are called to do, we open ourselves up to experience what only God can do. You may be preparing spices, but God is preparing miracles. *love this ! He is a God of miracles*

TABLE TALK

Luke 24 tells us that the women went to the tomb in the early morning. Do you start your mornings with seeking Jesus? Seeking Him first is part of what we are all called to do. In Psalm 5:3, David sings, "In the morning, Lord, you hear my voice; in the morning I lay my requests before you and wait expectantly."

Examine your morning routine. Do you lay down your requests before Jesus and wait expectantly? Of course, God wants us to seek Him throughout the day, but I think there's something special about starting your day with Him. In another Psalm, we read, "I wait for the Lord more than watchmen wait for the morning, more than watchmen wait for the morning" (Psalm 130:6). Watchmen were known to keep an eye out for danger over the city walls. They had to be alert, wait, and watch through long hours in the night. The dawn of a new day brought relief. The danger of the night eventually led to a new day.

There is a sign of promise that comes with every new day. It's like God saying, "I'm not finished yet." Practice waking up and starting your day with Jesus. Bring Him your tired heart and wait expectantly for Him, as the watchmen wait for the morning.

Give God Room To Show Himself Faithful

Luke 22:7-20

The disciples were about to have their last meal with Jesus before He died on the cross. It happened to be during Passover and Jesus asked His friends to prepare the meal. When they asked where they would prepare it, Jesus told them not to worry, for there was a man in the city who would direct them to a large and spacious room. We know it as the upper room. It's funny how we always have questions, and Jesus already has all the solutions and answers. The disciples didn't need to worry about how and where. Jesus simply asked them to prepare the meal.

Once Jesus came and reclined at the table, He broke the unleavened bread and said, "This is my body, which is given for you. Do this in remembrance of me" (Luke 22:19). And then He took the cup of wine and told them to drink it in remembrance of the blood He would pour out for them. I assume the disciples may have been a little puzzled. Where was Jesus going with this analogy? While the disciples were preparing a Passover meal, Jesus was preparing to give His life for them...for us.

All these preparations happening in a single upper

room. This room would also be the room in which Jesus washed His disciples' feet, where His disciples gathered after His ascension into Heaven, and where the Holy Spirit came down on the day of Pentecost. A very spacious room just outside of the old city of Jerusalem made way for God to move in miraculous ways.

Wherever God places us in seasons of preparation, be confident that He has called you to that very place. Jesus is present in our upper rooms, and when we give Him space, we are inviting Him in to do what only He can do. When we give Him room, He speaks. When we give Him room, He washes our dirty, tired feet. When we give Him room, He pours out His spirit on us. Give Him room. Give Him room to show Himself faithful because He is.

TABLE TALK

Are you preparing for harvest? Pentecost is the Greek name for what the Jewish people called "The Feast of Harvest." You can read more about this feast throughout the Old Testament in Exodus 23, Exodus 24, Leviticus 16, Numbers 28, and Deuteronomy 16. The Holy Spirit came on that sacred feast, but the disciples made room for Him. How can you make room for your harvest? I know for me, writing this devotional is what He's been asking me to prepare in this season, and at times I have struggled to be obedient. I don't always feel like writing encouraging spiels, such as about waiting on God, but I have to trust that His faithfulness meets me on the other side of my preparation because He is preparing something, too. The disciples were in for some big surprises. Little did they know that the upper room would become such a vital part of the early church. Harvest comes because we do our part and let God do His. We'll talk more about the concept of harvest in the coming weeks, but for now, just keep your heart expectant.

day 7

Christian's Story

I got pregnant in April of 2003. My husband was so happy as this would have been his first child. After we went to our first ultrasound, I knew something was wrong. I had my husband and my two daughters from a previous marriage with me so they could see the baby on the monitor. The technician started asking me several questions and I knew something was wrong, especially since she did not show me the monitor. We later discovered that we had lost our baby due to Trisomy 22. The DNA showed that the baby would have been a girl – Rebecca. We were devastated! My husband and I wanted to have a baby, but we were having a difficult time getting pregnant again. We prayed for months and waited with faith at God's table. Finally, in January of 2004, we were ecstatic to find out that we were pregnant with a baby boy. However, it was a high-risk pregnancy due to Placenta previa. I hemorrhaged throughout the pregnancy, so they decided to admit me to the hospital at 22 weeks until the baby's birth. Here I was again, waiting for almost 3 months, praying that I could deliver a healthy baby boy at full term. Every time I had a hemorrhage, they'd have to wheel me to the maternity high-risk area and give me magnesium sulfate which made me feel limp like a wet noodle. I couldn't eat, get up from bed, wear my contact lenses – nothing. I didn't even have strength to scoot myself up in bed. There were times where I wondered how long I would have to go through feeling that way. But I kept saying that I was staying strong for my son, so I waited. Christian was born on July 23, 2004 at 32 weeks and was in the NICU for 5 weeks, but he was healthy!

Fast forward 11 years to November of 2015, Christian was sent home from school with a high fever. We took him to doctor the next day, because the fever would not go down. When they pressed down on his right abdomen, he complained of extreme pain. They told us to take him to AI Children's Hospital immediately to be checked for appendicitis. After a host of tests, scans, and x-rays, we were told that our 11-year-old son had cancer (Ewing's Sarcoma with metastasis to his lungs). We were absolutely devastated. Why would he be taken away from us after all we went through to have him? I stopped asking questions and started to pray. The prayers of friends and family, and the faith that I have in God carried me through this very difficult time. Aside from that, Christian's positive attitude, wonderful sense of humor, and most of all the faith I saw him demonstrate during that time was humbling. Even through all the fears and questions going through his 11-year-old mind, he'd pray, and he'd accept prayer over him. Was this what God was preparing in heaven's kitchen? Was it the faith of an 11-year-old boy that would encourage and comfort so many? After 4 months of chemo treatments, many hospital stays, several blood transfusions, and a stem cell harvest, the tumor had reduced in size in such a dramatic way that the doctors would be able to remove the remaining tumor and part of his iliac crest without needing to have any bone replacement. After the surgery, we were told he was in remission! He finished his chemo treatment on August 29, 2016.

He'd still have regular blood tests, CT scans, and MRI's every 3 months. At the end of June 2018, he had what would have been his last CT Scan and MRI before transitioning to x-rays every 3-5 months. The scans showed something questionable in the marrow and the doctors ordered a more detailed MRI of Christian's leg, arm and spine. Needless to say, I started to worry, but tried to remain calm and faithful. On July 3, 2018, I got the dreaded call from the doctor. Christian had AML Leukemia. Treatment needed to start immediately. I dropped everything, ran to my car, and broke down! I cried, I yelled, and I kept asking "Why?!" This diagnosis was more devastating than the first. Prior to starting the treatment, he needed to get a CT scan of his chest. Doctors saw something on or near the chest wall that needed to be biopsied, so off he went to surgery. The results came back a couple of days later and not only did he have AML, he also had a relapse of the Ewing's Sarcoma. To make matters worse, there was no protocol for treatment. I didn't think I could handle any more! We had a family meeting that afternoon where we were told that treating AML as secondary cancer would be very tough. The survival rate for secondary AML was 15-20% but treating two cancers was going to be even tougher. One of the options that was offered was to take him home – keep him comfortable. I told them that that was not an option. The only question my son asked was, "Is it treatable?" He wasn't giving up and neither was I. During this heart-wrenching time, we were showered with so much love and so many prayers. I'll never forget the day that I looked outside the window of my son's hospital room and saw a large group from my church family gathered in the lawn, all praying at the same time we prayed in our room. I'll never forget the week after Christian's transplant when he was in excruciating pain. He'd call me over to his bedside and ask me to pray for him right then and there so that he could drink a sip of water without pain. What was God preparing in the kitchens of heaven during that time? Was it unity in prayer, an outpouring of love, increased faith for me and for Christian, new friendships, renewed friendships, and new talents (Christian learned how to play the ukulele during this time)? God is always doing more than you think and He carried us and gave us strength in what seemed like a never-ending waiting room. But miracles do happen. Christian is currently in remission and we continue to thank God for the blessings that He gives us daily.

PINEAPPLE stuffing

INGREDIENTS

½ cup Margarine
1 cup Sugar
4 Eggs
1 20 oz can Crushed Pineapples (drained)
5 slices White Bread (Cubed)

DIRECTIONS

1. Preheat oven at 350 degrees.
2. Melt the butter.
3. In a mixing bowl, mix all ingredients together (except the bread).
4. Place cubed bread into a baking pan and pour the mixture over the bread.
5. Bake at 350 degrees for 1 hour until toothpick comes out clean.
6. * Use 9 x 13 pan when doubling the recipe.

week 2

NOTHING IS EVER
WASTED
IN GOD'S KITCHEN

Bruised Apples

You've kept track of all my wandering and my weeping.
You've stored my many tears in your bottle—not one will be
lost. For they are all recorded in your book of remembrance.
Psalm 56:8

P salm 56 says that God collects our tears in His
bottle. If that's the case, God collects my tears in
barrels. I'm not ashamed to admit that I cry a lot.
Whether I am happy or sad, tears are a normal form of
expression for me. It has taken me quite a while to embrace
that part of me. I used to feel embarrassed or weak if others
caught me crying. But in the Bible, people are no strangers
to tears. Even Jesus wept. And everyone in the Bible also
experiences some degree of pain. Have you realized that?
No one's life in God's Word is exempt from it, not even
Jesus'.

The Bible, however, does not always express how the
person is processing those emotions internally. The
comforting thing is that pain is something we can all relate
to, and the beautiful thing about pain is that it is never
wasted when it is in God's hands.

I remember watching a cooking show once, and a chef
was talking about how her grandmother had grown up on
an apple orchard. Every day, there would be bruised and

broken apples that had fallen on the ground. Even though her family couldn't sell those apples, they didn't let them go to waste. They made apple sauce, apple pie, apple dumplings, apple butter...you get the picture. They took something broken that others may have thrown away and made it something wonderful for all to indulge in.

The brokenness we feel does not go to waste, not in God's kitchen. He does much more with our pain than we think He does. And when we fall, He doesn't overlook us. He picks us up and says, "I can make something out of this brokenness." I know it's hard when our hearts are burdened with pain, but something is exciting about knowing that all things are working together for our good. Some of God's greatest recipes come from deep places of pain that have been stirred with a thousand tears.

TABLE TALK

One person in the Bible who was really good at expressing his feelings is King David. Last week, we read about how David remained still at the sight of his enemies. This week, we are introduced to a David who let fear lead the way for a moment. He went through extreme highs and extreme lows, but he always came back to the fact that God was and always would be faithful. This was the difference between him and Saul.

Both were imperfect, but David always bounced back to who God was. Scripture states that Psalm 56 was written in the period of David's life where he was captured in Gath. This was enemy territory and Goliath's hometown. David had been fleeing Saul who was out to kill him. Read 1

Samuel 21:10-12. Clearly, this time was a low point for David.

He had traded the Promised Land for Philistine territory because he was afraid. Even the Philistines knew who he was and the power he held. Isn't it crazy how our own enemies can know our identity better than we do? Saul knew, which is why he was out to kill David. The Philistines knew, too. Our enemies know we are a force to be reckoned with, even when our fear is clouding the awareness of our identity.

Have you ever tried to flee out of fear from where God planted you? How do you identify with David in this story? What does David do in Psalm 56 to set his sight back on his faithful God?

Yes, tried to leave Dallas when it wasn't time yet ♡
It's easy to let fear creep in.
I had this with Zack & Elie when everything went downhill but I had to pick myself back up & get & come back STRONGER
♡ PRAISE HIM ♡
He is our promise keeper

Through Thorns And Trees

John 11:1-27

We will camp in John 11 for the next few days. Most of us are familiar with the story of Jesus raising Lazarus from the dead, but what were the moments like leading up to that miracle? Jesus waited to come to Bethany even though He knew Lazarus was dying (John 11:6). Mary and Martha waited for Jesus to come and heal Lazarus, but He never showed up, at least, not when they wanted Him to. When Jesus finally arrived, Lazarus had already been in the tomb for four days. Can you imagine what was going through Mary and Martha's minds? Where was Jesus? Didn't He love them? If He loved them so much as the scripture says, why would He make them wait in despair like that? Why would He let His friend die?

Like many of us in seasons of waiting, we can be overtaken by questions and those questions soon turn into doubts about the nature and character of God. With our physical sight, we can't really understand why God would let Lazarus die, but with Heaven's vision, we realize that the whole thing was a set up for a greater miracle. Jesus could have healed Lazarus before he died because everyone already knew Jesus had the power to heal people. Instead

He showed up and showed off by raising a dead man from the grave.

Lazarus' resurrection was a beautiful foreshadowing of what was to come because soon after, Jesus would also die and be raised to life again. While Mary and Martha were waiting for Jesus to show up, He already had a plan to bring Lazarus back, but He would do it in His timing and in His way, a way that no human could have fathomed because His ways are higher than our ways.

Isaiah 55 not only describes the unfathomable ways God works beyond our understanding, but also promises that His word will always achieve its purpose. When Jesus said at the beginning of the story in John 4, "Sickness will not end in death," He meant it. It didn't matter what the process of fulfilling that promise looked like. His Word would not return void.

His Word sings the song of thorn bushes being replaced with giant sequoias. Jesus is our giant sequoia, our awestriking strong tower, and shelter who is alive and well. He didn't just hang on a tree, covered in thorns. Three days had passed before He rose as Calvary's sequoia. He accomplished exactly what He said He would.

TABLE TALK

If you want to seep into more of God's faithfulness, I encourage you to meditate on Isaiah 55. It's an invitation to the hungry, the thirsty, all of us. How is God speaking to your heart when you read the words, "Come, buy wine and milk without money and without cost."? Acquiring blessings without working for them is yet another way God works in ways different than our own. We're not used to receiving things without purchasing them first. But Jesus paid the ultimate price, so we wouldn't have to bear the weight of our own sin, and with that payment, He invited us to taste and see His goodness forever in eternity.

At His Feet, Jesus Weeps

John 11:28-37

Of the three times that Mary of Bethany is mentioned in the Bible, she is found at the feet of Jesus. When Jesus visits Mary and Martha, Mary is at Jesus' feet. When Jesus was awaiting His crucifixion, Mary anointed His feet with oil to prepare Him for burial. And now, when Mary sees Jesus after her brother Lazarus had died, she falls at His feet and says, *"Lord, if you had been here, my brother would not have died"* (John 11:32).

Mary loved Jesus and she was always at His feet, but even Mary struggled to understand what Jesus was doing. She had spent so much time with Him, but still could not fully grasp the way that He worked. We too can spend all of our free time with Jesus, worship Him throughout the day, do His will, pray without ceasing, and still not fully grasp the way He works. Philippians 4:7 says that the peace of God surpasses all understanding, so why do we act surprised when we don't understand what He's doing?

I don't know all the answers as to why Jesus doesn't always show up when we want Him to and not knowing frustrates me the same way it probably frustrates you. Maybe you are overwhelmed with your own thoughts and questions in this season. But we can take comfort in knowing that even with our questions and tears, Jesus is deeply moved when we are at His feet. That's what happened with Mary. And it led to the shortest verse in the Bible- Jesus wept. God does not delight in our grief, our doubts, or our anxieties. Even when He knows greater is coming, He still weeps with us. Our brokenness pains Him. Think about that for a minute. Jesus wept with Mary even though He knew Lazarus would be raised to life again in a matter of minutes. He feels our pain, and he also grieves the fact that our human condition doesn't make it easy to choose faith beyond what our eyes can see.

TABLE TALK

---

① Where are you currently in your walk with the Lord? ② Have you laid your burdens down at Jesus' feet? The thoughts that weigh heavy on your heart, have you gone to Him with them? Talk to Him openly. Journal if that's easier but create a dialogue with Him. He is not intimidated by our pain or our tears.

① close relationships but want to make sure I spend more quality time w/ Him

② · I believe so - learning to be more vulnerable with God & to tell Him that I am disappointed for certain things

③ yes I believe so

start journaling more

Jesus Raises Lazarus

John 11:25, 38-44, Genesis 15:6, Romans 4:17-25

Continuing with the story of Lazarus, still deeply troubled, Jesus comes to the tomb. He knew what He was about to do, but the people around Him had no clue. As close of a friend as Martha was to Jesus, even she had her doubts when Jesus told them to move the stone.

Jesus said to her, "Did I not say to you that if you believe you would see the glory of God?" The word I want to focus on here is "believe." Believe- to hold on with complete assurance of what you cannot see.

Amid pain and trials, it's hard to believe that God is faithful or to believe that He's even there at all. But believing, against all hope is what perfects faith. Let's jump to an Old Testament story really quick to prove my point.

Genesis 15:6 says, *"By faith, Abraham believed God and it was credited to him as righteousness."* Abraham had received a promise from God that he would be the father of many nations while he and his wife were old and unable to bear children. The chances of them starting a family at their age was slim. Yet, against all hope, Abraham believed, and because of his faith, he saw the glory of God. He saw his promise fulfilled.

The same is true for us when we believe that Jesus died and rose again so that we may have new life. Abraham believed the God who *"gives life to the dead and calls those things which do not exist as though they did"* (Romans 4:17). The glory of God is revealed to us when we believe, even in the middle of our pain. Our belief in Him is not wasted. If we choose faith, He will prove himself faithful. Lazarus was raised from the dead. Jesus was raised from the dead and if we believe, our hopeless souls are raised from death into eternal life, too. To believe is to come fully alive.

TABLE TALK

Martha had her doubts even though she heard Jesus say her brother would rise again. When Jesus told her to remove the stone, her first response was basically, "Are you sure? He's going to smell pretty bad" (author's paraphrase). What stone are you letting hold you back from experiencing the glory of God? Is it your unbelief? Is it your lack of understanding that God works in mysterious ways? Is it your anxiety about what is to come if you do what He says? Are you afraid He will disappoint you? Determine the stones that are in your way and then ask God to help you remove them from your life.

What are some stones in my life
that hold me back
○ disappointment
○ fear
○ judgement

day 5

Jesus Uses Pain As A Means To
Bring Him All the Glory

John 11:37, Psalm 42

W hen Lazarus died, people surrounded Mary and Martha, and some of them didn't have consoling and encouraging words for the circumstance at hand. Some of them said, "Couldn't He who opened the blind man's eyes also have kept this man from dying?" (John 11:37) They mistook Jesus' tears for powerlessness. We are so quick to blame God when we do not understand the pain we are going through. This one verse led me to Psalm 42:3 which reads, *"My tears have been my food day and night, while they continually say to me, 'Where is your God?'"* While waiting for God at His table, do you ever feel like the only thing you've been feeding on is your tears? And meanwhile, people around you are wondering where this God of yours is.

I love this psalm because it shares the vulnerability of someone who is overtaken by sadness, yet still longs for God. The Psalmist knows that God is good. He mixes two ingredients in this psalm- his mind and his heart. He knows the truth about God's goodness, but he feels a deep sadness as he waits for God to show up.

The psalm ends with, *"Why am I so depressed? Why this turmoil within me? Put your hope in God, for I will still praise Him, my Savior and my God.*" He is choosing to push through his feelings and what others are saying by praising God and putting his hope in Him.

In seasons of waiting, often the battle is in our minds. We have so many questions. We go back to that cold, dark hospital waiting room I mentioned at the beginning of this devotional. Then, we get anxious when we don't see God moving. We confuse our lack of vision for God's indifference, just like the people who didn't understand why Jesus let Lazarus die. But the glory comes when Jesus turns the situation around. When our hope seemingly dies, it allows God to resurrect it for His glory.

TABLE TALK

Where do you need resurrection power today? Does your hope seem dead? Do your dreams seem to be far out of reach? Write your own psalm or song to the Lord, letting Him know exactly where you need new life today.

He Sets A Table

John 10:7-11, Psalm 23

J esus- our Good Shepherd, who lays down His life so that we may have life more abundantly. Jesus uses John 10 to describe the utmost dedication and love He has for us- His sheep. A good shepherd never leaves his sheep, for there is a thief out to kill, steal and destroy every dream, hope, and ounce of joy in our lives. 1 Peter 5:8 states that the devil prowls around like a roaring lion looking for someone to devour.

Knowing that the enemy is on the prowl doesn't mean we should feed that fear though. We have a Shepherd who longs to give us abundant life. Jesus reassures us in His Word that when we follow Him, He will lead us to pastures of abundance and flourishing life where we can feed on His goodness and truth.

John 10 is not the only place in scripture where God is mentioned as our Good Shepherd. David poetically proclaims in the first line of Psalm 23, *"The Lord is my shepherd...I lack nothing. He makes me lie down in green pastures, he leads me beside quiet waters, he refreshes my soul."* I encourage you to read this Psalm line by line and soak in it. He makes us lie down in green pastures. Jesus calls us to rest in Him... *"You prepare a table before me in the presence of my enemies."* (Psalm 23:5) Do you remember reading about this verse in Week 1? When our pain, anxiety, and fears surround us, our God invites us to feast with Him at His table. Sitting at His table is how we fight our battles. It's as if He's saying, "Forget about it. Come share a meal with Me, instead."

In the same verse, David declares, *"He anoints my head with oil."* Sheep are easy victims for pests like lice, flies, and ticks; therefore, oil would keep these pests away from crawling into their eyes and ears and eating away at their brain. Without the oil, these pests can irritate a sheep to the point of breaking its own skull to seek relief from these brain-eating parasites.

The enemy is seeking to do the same thing to our minds. If he can fill our heads with parasitic lies and fears, he knows he can steal our joy and even our life. For this reason, we need to protect our minds with the oil of the Lord, His Holy Spirit, and know that His goodness and mercy follow us all the days of our lives. We're going to feel surrounded by a lot of lies, fears, and seemingly insurmountable obstacles, but we can't quit. Because God not only surrounds us-, He also surrounds the enemy that surrounds us, and somehow, He sets a table in the middle of that mess.

TABLE TALK

Recount a time when Jesus set a table for you in the presence of your enemies. Can you see now as you look back that He was surrounding your situation the entire time? In what ways does Jesus provide abundant life for you in the middle of a circumstance that is trying to steal your joy?

August 2019 - hardest month of my life
Kristina had a ticket for me
for Propel Conference
Sep 2016 - felt hopeless but God
showed up in my prayers
& gave me a vision to move on

H eaven's kitchen...boy, has the Lord been busy cooking in my life. My adoption story actually started 34 years ago. My birth mother found herself pregnant with twins. She knew she couldn't care for us, but the Lord placed in her path a couple who longed to be parents. My twin brother and I were adopted in 1985. We grew up in a loving Christian home where adoption was never a secret or taboo subject for us. I knew from a very young age that I wanted to adopt a child also.

Fast forward many years and shortly after the birth of my first son, I went into heart failure and was told I would never be able to carry another child. My husband and I knew then the Lord had concreted His plan of adoption in our lives. Adoption was never our plan B though. We always planned on adopting; we just didn't know when. The Lord did though.

When our son turned two, we decided to start the adoption process. We were matched fairly quickly with a birth mom and off we went in planning for our daughter to be born. Only, nine months later around the time we were expecting this new baby girl, the bottom dropped out below us. Because of a string of poor choices from the birth mother, the baby we longed to hold, was no longer going to be possible for us. We went from anticipation and joy to hopelessness and broken hearts overnight.

We didn't understand why the Lord would take us up to that point, to leave us broken-hearted and confused. Even so, we still trusted Him, even though we knew He could have changed the outcome. We had seen Him faithful in our lives before, and we knew we would see it again, even with tear-stained faces.

We knew that He had a plan for us; we just didn't know what it was. We spent months grieving the loss of the baby girl we longed to love and parent. We often times wondered, "How long?" Then, seven months after the failed adoption, we got a call out of the blue that there had been a "stork drop" at the hospital. A baby boy. He was one day old at the time and our adoption attorney asked us if we wanted to adopt him. We did!

We couldn't believe what had just happened, and two days later we went to the hospital to meet our son. He looked just like our four-year-old, down to a matching dimple in his chin. He was wholly ours. When we had the failed adoption and our hearts were shattered, we had no idea that the Lord already knew this baby boy was in his birth mother's womb, being perfectly knit to be our son. We had no idea, but He did.

He had already restored all the locusts had eaten and gave us more than we ever hoped or prayed for. He gave us a perfect baby boy who looks just like us, who is easy going and sweet, who has chubby cheeks and curly hair. He knew we needed this baby, and this baby needed us.

When the storms started raging and life got hard, we didn't know the sweet things the Lord was cooking in Heaven's kitchen for us, but because of His love and grace, we did know what it was like to be cared for and loved on while we waited at His table for the feast He had coming. We never went without, He cared for us even when we struggled to pray and commune with Him. Waiting expectantly for the Lord can be hard at times, but when you get to see what He's prepared for you, you realize how very worth it, the wait was.

& patient

BANANA pudding

INGREDIENTS

16 ounce Instant Vanilla Pudding
1 ½ cup Milk
1 can Eagle Milk
1 8 ounce Cool Whip
1 box Vanilla Wafers
Bananas

DIRECTIONS

1. Mix together milk and pudding on low speed for about 2 minutes.
2. Blend in Eagle Milk.
3. Fold in Cool Whip.
4. In 9x13 dish, put a layer of Vanilla Wafers, layer of sliced bananas, then ½ pudding mixture. Repeat. Chill.

week 3

THIS ISN'T AN EASY BAKE OVEN

Day 1 - Strong Faith And Patient Endurance

For God, the Faithful One is not unfair. How can he forget the work you have done for him? He remembers the love you demonstrate as you continually serve his beloved ones for the glory of his name. But we long to see you passionately advance until the end and you find your hope fulfilled. So don't allow your hearts to grow dull or lose your enthusiasm, but follow the example of those who fully received what God has promised because of their strong faith and patient endurance.
Hebrews 6:10-12 TPT

H ave you ever been so hungry that you rummage through your fridge and pantry, only to find nothing but scraps of junk food and leftovers? But because you are so hungry, you eat what you can find anyway. You eat that microwaveable popcorn that's been in the pantry for two years, you eat that Halloween candy from Lord knows when, or you eat the random mashup of leftovers that are taking up room in your fridge. Now, you're full, but you're not fulfilled. In fact, you feel pretty lousy.

We act the same way in our walk with God. We want convenience. We live in a microwave culture, but we crave five-star restaurant results. God loves us too much to give us something before it's time for us to have it. Envision in your mind what your ideal four-course meal would look like. Now, try to recount all the steps it would take to create that meal. Not only do you need to prepare the meal, but you need to purchase the ingredients. And where did the ingredients come from? Did they just sprout up from the earth in a day? Does chocolate cake ever fall from the sky? If you have ever cooked anything, then you are aware of the process. And if you've been in the kitchen for any length of time, then you've also seen what happens when you don't cook something long enough, or you cook something for too long.

The good news is that God is never early, or late, but I heard once that He is simply last minute. This week, I want us to focus on what our hearts look like when we're patient versus impatient with God. God is used to His children growing through seasons that test our patience and His Word is filled with stories that testify to what patient endurance looks like. Hebrews 6:12 reminds us that strong faith and patient endurance work together to cultivate God's purpose in our lives. Are we activating both of those practices in our daily walk with Him?

TABLE TALK

Would you consider yourself a patient person? Some of us may be more patient than others, but we all, even Jesus, can have our patience stretched. Read Matthew 4:1-4. Jesus was tempted in the wilderness where He was most vulnerable. He was hungry, and the devil offered Him bread. The enemy will attack you where you are most vulnerable. He knows where to hit you.

What are your vulnerable areas? It's not a sin to struggle with weakness, but we need to practice living by God's Word and recognizing the enemy when He comes for the very fruit God is producing in our lives.

- patience
- getting caught up in past

An Easy Bake Oven

Genesis 2:16-17, Genesis 3:5

W hen I was a kid, I loved playing "house." I spent much of my early childhood "cooking" in my toy kitchen and serving play-dough dinners to my family, so naturally, I wanted an Easy Bake Oven. I really wanted an Easy Bake Oven. I was raised by a Latin mom who cooked dinner almost every night so in her eyes, an Easy Bake Oven was a waste of money. "Why would I get you that when we have a real oven that can make real food?" were some of the words she would say whenever I brought the subject up around Christmas and my birthday. Luckily, I had gone to my friend's house one day and she had one. I can't remember what we baked exactly, but I remember thinking, "This doesn't look or taste as great as it appears on the commercials."

The moral to my Easy Bake heartbreak story is this: we are drawn to instant gratification. If something looks good, we want it, and we want it now. We want possessing the Promised Land to be easy. We want it to be quick, and we want it to look like everything we've pictured, in our timing and in our own way. Eve is a prime example of this mindset.

Eve was so focused on what God told her not to have, that she missed everything He wanted to give her: an abundant and beautiful life in the garden. God told Adam and Eve that they could eat from any tree except the tree of the knowledge of good and evil. He gave them freedom before He gave them any restrictions. He was protecting them from what was less than His best. But when Eve saw that the fruit from the tree was "desirable to the eyes" and good for wisdom (Genesis 3:6), she settled for death instead of life. To this very day, we are paying the consequences for her distrust in God.

I know now that my mom was not being mean by not buying me an Easy Bake Oven. In fact, I grew up my whole life with more than I ever wanted or asked for. I was also raised with a mom who made sure I always went to bed with a warm meal in my stomach.

God is no different. He wants us to trust that He has good things for us. We cannot forget God's goodness because we are so focused on the one thing He's not giving us. What He is preparing for us doesn't just look good, it is good. And good things take time. His promises don't come in an Easy-Bake Oven, so leave it alone. Don't touch it. Don't open the oven prematurely. Let the fragrance and warmth of what He's preparing fill you with hope as you trust in Him.

TABLE TALK

Eve's lack of trust caused her to take matters into her own hands. She grabbed hold of the fruit, but more than that, she grabbed hold of the lie that God was keeping something from her. Have you ever wrestled with that lie before? Express your heart to God. He's not mad at you for feeling that way but identify the lies you've believed about Him and combat them with His truths. God is a giver. Every good and perfect gift is from above (James 1:17). What are some instances in your life where God has been generous to you?

My job, my promotions, meeting all these amazing people already here in Tampa, DN, friends all over the world my family

Don't Drink The Soup

Genesis 25:27-34, Hebrews 12:16 (MSG)

We've probably all heard about the patriarchs of our faith: Abraham, Isaac, and Jacob. And we have a bowl of bean chili to credit for that. You see, Isaac and Rebekah had twins, Esau and Jacob. They literally fought in the womb. Esau was the oldest, an expert outdoorsman who probably would have enjoyed Bass Pro Shops if he lived in today's world. Jacob was the younger of the two, and he stayed home. I can imagine him probably enjoying the Food Network with his mother, Rebekah, who preferred him to his older brother, Esau. Although Jacob was quieter, he was not stupid. He manipulated his older brother into selling him his birthright for a simple cup of soup. In this period of time, when a man died, his oldest son would inherit twice as much as the younger. The birthright was not only a title, but also a blessing, one that Esau didn't care for in a moment of weakness.

He had been working out in the fields and came home to see Jacob had whipped up some dinner. When he asked his younger brother for some, Jacob took advantage of Esau and replied, *"First sell me your birthright"* (Genesis 25:31). Esau dramatically responded making the point to question what good was his birthright when he was dying of starvation.

Don't we get a little dramatic in the heat of the moment? We're so hangry and caught up in the desires of our flesh, that we forget that God has so many beautiful gifts He intends to give us. The blessing and the birthright were intended for Esau, but his impatience cost him a lifetime of regret. He traded the ultimate blessing for what he could get in that moment...soup. Esau's trade sounds silly, but how many times has our hunger led us astray? How many times have we settled for fast food when we could have had a home-cooked meal? How many times have we settled for junk food out of convenience even though we know it's not remotely beneficial to us? We not only settle with food, but also with God.

The issue isn't that God doesn't want to bless us. The issue is our impatience. In a moment of exhaustion and hunger, Esau couldn't remotely feel the weight of God's Promise for his future. He felt only his hunger. Esau couldn't see God's blessing in his future. All he could see was what was right in front of him- a bowl of soup. In Hebrews 12:16, we are reminded of Esau's mistake as a warning and encouragement. We are warned to be careful about what you do when you're hungry. Don't trade your blessing for a bowl of soup. The encouragement is this: when we remain steadfast on the Perfecter of our faith in times of deep hunger pains, He will sustain us. If we act in strong faith and patient endurance (Hebrews 6:12), He will give us the grace to finish the race and we not only make it, but we win everything He intended to give us.

TABLE TALK

The drama between Esau and Jacob didn't stop with the birthright. Jacob was back at his old tricks when he stole Esau's blessing before Isaac died in Genesis 28. By this point, Esau was after Jacob's life. Thankfully, God's grace worked out Jacob's purpose, but it didn't come without a life full of lessons. Read Genesis 28:10-17.

As Jacob was running from his own brother, God met him in the middle of nowhere. In the middle of our mess, God is faithful to meet us where we are. We may not even be aware of His presence, but He is there. In the middle of our mistakes, when it seems like the promises of God are far removed from our life, God whispers to us in dreams and visions.

What are some ways God has spoken to you when you were in the middle of nowhere or in the middle of a big mess you didn't know how you were going to get out of? My prayer for us is that we recognize that He is with us in every place of our lives and He will make good on every promise He has made.

→ day before I gave my life to God

Making Messes

Genesis 15:1-6, Genesis 16:1-5

Esau isn't the only person in the Bible to take matters into his own hands. In fact, his grandfather, Abraham, did the same thing. Isn't it comforting to know that Abraham who is known as the Father of our faith, was just as broken as we are?

God spoke the same promise over him time after time. In Genesis 12:2, God says, "I will make of you a great nation." Five verses later, He says, "To your offspring, I will give this land." In Genesis 13:15, "For all the land you see, I will give to you and your offspring." The list of repeated promises goes on throughout the heartbeat of Genesis. God was gracious enough to keep reminding Abraham of His promise. All he had to do was wait for the appointed time for God to bring it to pass.

But just like all Esau could see was what was right in front of him, Abraham and Sarah saw that they were old. How was she going to conceive a child? So, she did what we all do; she tried to come up with a solution. God never intended for Sarah to have to come up with a solution. Her job was to trust God with what was impossible for her to do on her own. Instead, she told Abraham to sleep with her servant, Hagar. Hagar later birthed Ishmael, and although this whole scheme was Sarah's idea, she hated Hagar for birthing their false promise. Hagar was left feeling alone. Ishmael was destined to have his hand against everyone (Genesis 16:12).

When we take matters into our own hands, we are destined for disappointment. This is why God commands us to "be still." It's kind of like when you get ketchup on your shirt, and you know that if you try to wipe it off, you'll only make the stain bigger. God forbid we walk around with ketchup on our shirt. What do we do? We try to wipe it off anyway and guess what. We still have ketchup on our shirt. It's just bigger and messier and more noticeable than before. Awesome.

We are good at making messes, but God is so gracious. Even after Ishmael was born, God promised that Sarah would give birth to a son named Isaac within the year, and it was through Isaac that God would establish His covenant. God doesn't eliminate the mess we make, but He is faithful to keep His Promises. Even when we are faithless, He is faithful.

TABLE TALK

In Genesis 18, after Ishmael had already been born, Abraham was met by three men and it is understood that one of these "men" was the Lord, Himself. Abraham bowed low in their presence and was quick to prepare a hearty meal for them. He offered his very best to them and served them with fervor and sincerity. Abraham knew he was in the presence of God.

What can you offer to God as He meets you right where

you're at in a particular season? While they ate, he stood by them and that's when they asked about Sarah. It was then and there that God spoke to Abraham and let him know that within the year, at the appointed time, Sarah would have a son. Sarah was lurking in the background, catching wind of these three mysterious men having quite the chat with her husband. She laughed in disbelief. Her laugh was equivalent to saying, "Yeah right!"

One of my favorite Bible teachers, Beth Moore, made this profound statement on social media (of all places), and it has stayed with me when genuine laughter never seemed farther away: "Sarah, after the long-awaited Isaac was born: 'God has made laughter for me.' No one wants to need a miracle but oh the ridiculous joys of receiving one. Laughter never feels better to a set of lungs than when it belts out a benediction to years of tears. May God make you laugh."

Who knew someone could speak straight to your heart like that while mindlessly scrolling through the Internet? The name Isaac means, "laughter." Sarah's laughter went from one of pain to one of joy.

What are you hoping to laugh about in the future, my friend? As we wait for the appointed time, I pray we can laugh at the joy that is to come.

Dreams Are Not Microwaveable

Genesis 37-50, Genesis 37:1-8, Genesis 50:20, Romans 8:28

We've examined the life of two patriarchs of our faith this week, Abraham and Jacob (Israel), and today, we are going to dive into the story of Jacob's beloved son, Joseph. Joseph is one of my favorite people in the Bible, probably because he's a dreamer just like me.

Joseph was set apart and favored by his father, while equally hated by his brothers. He was deeply misunderstood and outcasted, but he remained steadfast in what God said, and that faith pulled Joseph through some of the lowest valleys in his life.

His brothers had reached their end with Joseph when he had a dream that they were bowing down to him, so long story short, they sold him into slavery and told their father he was killed. Joseph ended up in Egypt and through another series of unfortunate events, (which you can read about in Genesis 39), he ended up in prison. If I were Joseph, I'd definitely be asking God some questions. "Why did you give me those dreams if You weren't going to fulfill them? Did I even really hear from You? Why did You let this happen? Are You even there? How are my dreams ever going to come to pass while I am in this prison? Maybe I don't hear from God. I feel so stupid for believing I did." I can imagine I would be asking the same questions if I were Joseph.

During his time in prison, he was able to interpret two other prisoners' dreams, both of which came to pass. He didn't neglect his gift despite the disappointments he had faced. Thank God he didn't because two years later, the cupbearer whose dream Joseph interpreted told Pharaoh about his experience with this dreamer. Pharaoh was desperate for an interpretation of his own dreams, so he called for Joseph and because of his ability to interpret dreams, Joseph saved an entire people from famine. He also became the second most powerful man in all of Egypt.

As far as his brothers were concerned, his dream came to pass when they bowed down to him as they desperately sought food in Egypt during the famine. Forgiveness was celebrated as God used the most unfortunate of circumstances to fulfill His purpose. Joseph's dreams were always valid, even deep within prison walls. Just because a dream is revealed in faith doesn't mean it won't take time to be revealed in reality.

Joseph never gave up on the God who is faithful to fulfill the dreams He gives us. He remained faithful to God when he could have abandoned him. Joseph had every reason to be frustrated with God, but he continued to cultivate what God had given him while imprisoned. We need to use what we have wherever God has us and hold on to God for dear life until we see the fruit of our faithfulness. It doesn't matter how far off the path we have been thrown. God always finds a way and when He does, His goodness will bless our faith and the faith of those around us.

TABLE TALK

Joseph's story takes up a prominent place in Genesis. Thirteen detailed chapters are dedicated to revealing God's nature through his story. It is a narrative brimming with lessons in forgiveness, patience, righteousness, and God's character to work all things together for good. What part of Joseph's story speaks the most to you? Psalm 105:19 attests, "God's promise to Joseph purged his character until it was time for his dreams to come true." What is God purging in your character in this season of your life?

continue to stay faithful & keep in don't drift off

D patience

From Weeping To Eating

1 Samuel 1

Perhaps, one of my favorite Bible stories about a broken heart is the story of Hannah. Her fervent cries that ascended to the Lord in prayer reminded me that it is okay to feel deeply and the Lord welcomes us with open arms when we bring our pain to Him. Hannah and Peninnah were Elkanah's wives. However, Peninnah had children, but Hannah had not been able to conceive. Every year, this family traveled up to Shiloh to worship and offer a sacrifice up to God and every year, Peninnah taunted Hannah with the reality that she was barren. So much for a nice family vacation.

Year after year, Elkanah gave a portion of the sacrificial meal to Peninnah and her children, but he would give a double portion to Hannah because he loved her and knew she was in despair over her barrenness. But Hannah had no appetite. Elkanah questioned his worth to her since she was always depressed. All she could focus on was her broken heart and her many years of deferred hope. Isn't hard for us to focus on the blessings in front of us when all we can see is our unanswered prayers? On one trip, Hannah, unable to eat, got up from the table and went to pray. She prayed hard, asking God for a son. She had never been in physical labor, but Hannah found herself in spiritual labor, pushing in prayer until Heaven opened up.

Her passionate prayers got the attention of the priest, Eli, who thought she was drunk. After she explained her story, he blessed her and said, *"Go in peace. And may the God of Israel give you what you asked of him"* (1 Samuel 1:17). She got up, ate a good meal, and went on her way with peace and joy. One desperate prayer can open a door of praise. Within some time, God remembered Hannah and answered her long-standing prayer with Him.

God is not intimidated by our tears or fervent prayers. He hears the cries of our hearts, no matter how crazy we sound when we are crying out to Him. Elkanah went to Shiloh every year to present a sacrifice to the Lord, but this time, Hannah presented her own sacrifice. She promised if God gave her a son, she would dedicate him back to the Lord all the days of his life. Prayer opens up a way for God to work and it also changes the posture of our hearts. God wants our sacrifice, our surrender, and our burdens so we can get up, be filled, and eat, just like Hannah did after she finished praying. It is normal to lose our appetite for God when we're used to disappointment. It's normal to grow weary when it seems like everyone else is feasting on God's faithfulness except for you. But while we are crying out, God is still preparing the way in the kitchens of Heaven. Remember, God's answers don't come in a microwave or an Easy Bake Oven. It's sometimes years of prayer, tears, and surrender that bring forth the feast He is preparing.

TABLE TALK

When was the last time you cried out to God? Are you willing to surrender back to Him the very thing you desire most? Hannah wanted a son so badly she promised to dedicate him back to the Lord all the days of his life. That's exactly what she did when Samuel was born. After he was weaned, she took him back to Shiloh to be raised in the House of the Lord under Eli, the same priest who heard Hannah's cry. Samuel's name means, "God has heard."

What prayers are you believing God hears from you today? Imagine for a moment that God answers your petition. How would you dedicate that answered prayer back to the Lord?

- my future husband
- my family to have a relationship w/ God
- mission trip
- continued obedience, telling more people about my testimony to draw them close

day 7

Lisa's Story

Where do I even start? First of all, God is so good and so faithful. Knowing how God has totally changed my life for the better is an understatement. I gave my life to the Lord on March 12, 2017. It was the best decision I could have ever made. At that time, I was still married to my now ex-husband who was unfaithful and verbally abusive. Life was anything but easy at that time, especially with having none of my family living anywhere close to me nor living in this country.

Not knowing if I would still be able to stay in the United States after my divorce, was constantly on my mind, but I didn't give up. I cried out to Him every single night. I prayed BIG, especially after hearing a spectacular sermon in May of 2017. That sermon absolutely changed my prayer life! It taught me to ask BIG, it taught me that there are no prayers too big for our God. It taught me to wait and trust until God's answer comes. Whatever you are asking God for, He will deliver the answer when the time is right.

After my divorce was final in the summer of 2017, I was then able start the process to receive my green card, which at times left me with no hope but I always reminded myself to continue to pray, continue to stay plugged in, and to have tons of community surrounding me.

In November of 2017, my paperwork for my Green

Card was finally submitted, which was a relief but also a nerve-wracking experience. After that, tons of prayers followed. Fear definitely tried to creep in at times to remind me that if I get a "no" on my application, I would have to leave this country and go back to Austria at any time.

However, I didn't let fear take over. I continued to give it all to God and pray about my residency in the U.S. every single night. I also started traveling to Tampa, Florida for work more often. I remember the very first time I got there, I felt full peace. Nothing was worrying me anymore. At that point, I knew I wanted to live there one day. I fell more in love with it every single time I visited from Dallas.

Finally, in the summer of 2018, I decided to ask my boss if I could relocate. That conversation didn't go very well. I was extremely discouraged, hopeless and at the same time reminded that I might not even be able to stay in the U.S. anyways because I was still waiting on my Green Card.

I continued to get back up and reminded myself of the huge purpose God has set for me..I prayed about my desire to move to Tampa and my green card every single night. I knew God had placed these dreams on my heart, so I wanted to let God work it out if this is what He had for me.

However, one of the hardest challenges for me is being patient. I'm probably one of the most impatient people. Patience is not something I was born with, but I started to grow in that area more and more.

About a year had passed, and I still had no word on my United States residency. In November, I felt like God was telling me to pray for January 16 to receive my Green Card. I prayed for that date every single night. On January 11, I got an automatic email from immigration mentioning that my new card was ordered. I started crying when I found out about it. What was even more unreal was that on January

15, the day we had been praying for, my new Green Card, shipped! God is so incredibly faithful!

During this whole time we have been praying for Tampa too but nothing sparked or happened until after my company went through some change within management. I started feeling more peace about Tampa and in April I felt like it was time to ask my new boss about my potential real-location.

Well, let's just say this: Another prayer was answered. Without any problems, my biggest dream of living by the water in Florida was now becoming a reality. I moved to Tampa in the summer of 2019. God is so incredibly faithful and His timing is perfect.

WIENERSCHNITZEL MIT KARTOFFELSALAT
with potato salad

INGREDIENTS

3 pounds Veal or Chicken
7 ounces Flour
4 Eggs
7 ounces Bread Crumbs, dry, unseasoned
Splash of Milk
Splash of Canola Oil
Canola Oil, for frying
Salt and Pepper, for seasoning
2 pounds of Gold Potatoes
Medium-sized White Onion - half
White Wine Vinegar
Olive Oil
Fresh Chives
Cranberry Jam

DIRECTIONS

Wienerschnitzel:

1. Slice veal/chicken against the grain into 1/4-

inch rounds. Lightly pound until 2/8 of an inch thick (pounding will allow it to cook evenly, tenderize the meat and make it soufflé nicer).
2. Season with salt and pepper.
3. Beat egg with the splash of milk and drop of oil.
4. Dip the veal/chicken slices in flour, egg (beaten with splash of milk & drop of oil) and breadcrumbs. Shake off excess.
5. Heat oil until 350 degrees F. Add the meat slices and crisp under constant circular movement for 60 seconds. Remove from the oil. Pat dry and serve.

Potato Salad:

1. Place whole potatoes in a pot and cover with water. Bring the water to a boil over high heat. Reduce the heat and simmer the potatoes until just barely fork tender (10-15 min).
2. Once the potatoes are cooked, drain them and let them cool down.
3. While the potatoes are cooling, mix the vinegar, olive oil, salt, and pepper together in a small saucepan.
4. By now, the potatoes should be cool enough to handle. Peel and slice them into ¼ inch slices and place the sliced potatoes into a medium bowl.
5. Add the onions and sauce mixture. Mix well. Cover the bowl and let the potatoes stand for 1 hour to absorb the flavors.

6. Once the potatoes have rested, add the oil and mix well.
7. Sprinkle the freshly cut chives on top of the salad.
8. Serve immediately or refrigerate for 12-24 hours to let the flavors come together. Remove the potato salad from the refrigerator for at least 1 hour before serving to allow it to come to room temperature.

You can serve your Wienerschnitzel with potato salad and some cranberry jam as a sauce. Mahlzeit & guten Appetit!

week 4

A STIRRING HOPE

day 1

The Threshing Floor

*"A farmer went out to sow his seed. As he was scattering the
seed, some fell along the path; it was trampled on, and the
birds ate it up. Some fell on rocky ground, and when it came
up, the plants withered because they had no moisture. Other
seed fell among thorns, which grew up with it and choked the
plants. Still, other seed fell on good soil. It came up and
yielded a crop, a hundred times more than was sown."*
Luke 8:5-8 NIV

Where do we place our hope when we see no
signs of harvest? I believe God wants to root
our hope in a deeper place. Our hope is found
in God's Word. It's found in Jesus. (John 1:1) Maybe we
need to bury that hope deep in the soil of our hearts, but it
must be good and fertile soil. When God's Word falls on
rocky ground or among thorns, our hope cannot flourish,
and His Word cannot accomplish what it was meant to. We
know, based on Isaiah 55:10-11, that God fully intends to
fulfill His Word in our lives, but the condition of our heart
(the soil) is what limits the growth of the seed. On the flip
side of the quality of our soil, it can also act as a catalyst for
that seed to grow to its fullest capacity. What is the condition of your heart right now? Is God's Word buried deep in
your heart so that you can steward the harvest well when it

comes? Or are you filled with so much hopelessness and disappointment that God's Word can't even take root?

We need to check the condition of our soil if we are to reap a harvest, and when the harvest comes, we will need to do our part. In harvesting wheat, for example, the wheat berry must be separated from the hull and stem in a process called threshing. Then, the berries need to be separated from the chaff, which is then blown to the wind in a process called winnowing. A lot of work goes into harvesting a small berry that blesses so many people in a big way.

Many times, we want the harvest, but we don't want to put in the work to get there or the work it takes to sustain it. We want a breakthrough, but we're not willing to plant the seed. We want God to send the rain, but we don't want to cry out for it. We want the promise, but we don't want to get our hands dirty.

We need to learn the art of planting our hope and harvesting with patience. Harvest is a burden if you don't know what to do with it. All the wheat in the world would rot and go to waste if we didn't go through the threshing and winnowing, but after the process, comes a blessing. And just like God's Word goes forth into the earth and accomplishes the purpose in which He sent it, every seed that goes into fertile ground will grow in its time and fulfill its purpose.

TABLE TALK

Read the meaning behind the Parable of the Sower in Luke 8:11-15. Which condition of soil do you resonate with most?

There's rocky ground: Do you find joy in hearing God's *remember* Word, but find yourself struggling to believe it in times of trial and testing? You could be lacking a root system. What can you do to ensure you grow down some roots in God's Word? *get into His word more & have more quiet time w/Him*

There's thorny ground: Are you choked with the worries, riches, and pleasures of life? Are you constantly worried if God will come through for you, jumping from faith to doubt constantly? Read and memorize James 1:6-8 (NIV). Double-mindedness will produce no mature fruit. As for riches and pleasures, God desires for us to have abundance, but are you more focused on The Giver or the gift? What thorns do you need to cut out of your soil?

There's good ground: What does it mean to have an honest and good heart? What does it look like to hold on to God's Word in trying times? Read Psalm 1:1-3. This seed is the seed that will bear much fruit.

Barley Blessings

Ruth 1, Ecclesiastes 3:1-11

God brought Ruth and Naomi from famine to harvest, literally and figuratively. They went from lack to abundance. They both left Moab empty, broken, and missing pieces of themselves. They journeyed towards Bethlehem when Naomi learned that the famine was over in her native homeland. Little did she know that the famine in her life was ending as well. Every step towards Bethlehem was preparing them for the harvest God was preparing for them. Keep in mind that God was preparing all of this while Naomi was in bitter despair. While I am not encouraging us to be bitter in hard seasons, I am making a point to say that our God is so good that even if we only have enough faith to move one foot in front of the other, He is still faithful to bless us with a harvest. One step in obedience is a step in the right direction.

Ruth brought balance to her broken mother-in-law. Ruth remained steadfast under the trials they faced, and she was determined to get to God's intended destination, regardless of what was in store for her once she got there. This pairing is a powerful example of what it means to be surrounded by a good community, even if it's just one person. When we are hopeless, one person taking the next step with us is all we need to keep moving forward. Find those core people in your life. Encourage each other in times of lack and celebrate with one another in times of abundance. This is how Ruth and Naomi lived.

They walked together and arrived in Bethlehem just as the barley harvest was beginning, (Ruth 1:22). The detail of when they had arrived was the last sentence in the chapter. God wastes no details. I believe He wants us to know that when they arrived in Bethlehem was an important key to foreshadowing what would happen next in the story. If they had never followed God back home, they would have missed the barley harvest. If they missed the barley harvest, they would have missed Boaz who worked over the barley fields. I'm getting ahead of myself. But again, I will say, every step they took led them closer to a blessing they didn't see coming.

TABLE TALK

Maybe you feel a little bitter like Naomi these days. Who has been a "Ruth" in your life that has helped you put one foot in front of the other? Write them a letter, take them out for coffee, or find a unique way to show your appreciation for them. Some seasons would be impossible to go through without someone pointing you back to Jesus along the way. Are you a Ruth in anyone's life? How can you come alongside someone you care about and walk with them in their journey? Call a friend you know is going through a hard time and pray for them. Let them know you're with them. Walk forward together. Harvest is right around the corner.

day 3

Sowing Seeds

Ruth 2, Proverbs 31:15, Galatians 6:9

Not every season will be one of reaping, but in every season, we can sow seeds. No matter how weak we feel in our own strength, we have the glorious opportunity to make the most of the seeds we've been given. Ruth did. She didn't wait for someone to offer her a job. She didn't throw a pity party, saying, "I don't belong here. Becoming like these people is never going to work out for me." Instead, she asked if she could glean in the fields and collect leftover grain. This practice was common for the poor and foreigners in these days, for God's law commanded that the Hebrew people would let the poor gather their gleanings (Leviticus 23:22).

Ruth just so happened to be gleaning in the fields belonging to Boaz who was a Kinsman Redeemer in Naomi's family. A Kinsman Redeemer meant that if a wife in the family was left as a widow, he would commit to marry her and protect her. Neither Ruth nor Naomi knew whose field she was in at the time, but Boaz took notice of Ruth, who worked from early morning to evening, and when he found out who she was, he showed favor to her. He didn't lavish extra grace upon her because he was trying to impress her. He bestowed favor on her because of her noble charac-ter- her faithfulness to Naomi, and her willingness to embrace a land unknown to her.

Are we waking up with the same willingness to do what God has called us to do, even among difficult circum-stances? Are we so eager for the next season that we miss what we could be sowing in this season? I know for me, one of the biggest challenges I face is staying focused on the "here and now." All I see is where I want to be. By doing so, I waste valuable time moping in my current season. But Ruth got to work! She didn't have time to mope and by her actions, she positioned herself for the biggest blessing. I haven't quite mastered the art of embracing the present, but I believe that if we get to sowing the seeds God is calling us to sow in our current season, we will reap a harvest of blessing in the next season. It doesn't matter if you're watering those seeds with your tears. Every seed planted in God's hands will grow.

TABLE TALK

Seeds don't hold much value until they have been planted. When they are planted, not only do they produce fruit, but also they produce more seeds. Your obedience right now leads to generational blessing. What seeds are you holding in your hand that need to be planted? What work do you need to be doing to make sure that the seed is germi-nating in the ground? 1 Corinthians 3:9 says that we are co-laborers with Christ. One translation even calls us *"God's cultivated garden."* We definitely play a part in the story.

We'll talk more about that tomorrow, but God will bring the rain if we plant the seed. Journal about the seeds you are planting or have planted and write what you're going to do on your end to see that garden flourish.

day 4

Hope for Harvest

Ruth 3, Romans 5:3-5, Lamentations 3:21-33 (NLT)

The third chapter of Ruth is one of those chapters in the Bible that make you scratch your head and wonder what God is actually saying. On the surface, Naomi's plan for Ruth to go sleep secretly at Boaz's feet on the threshing floor, seems suggestive and risky. And while the author doesn't tell us why Naomi went about getting Boaz's attention in this way, we know that she intended to remind Boaz of his right to redeem Ruth. We can almost hear Naomi's confidence and hope as she tells Ruth what to do. She no longer sounds like the bitter woman she described herself as in the first chapter.

When plans haven't gone our way, the disappointment can breed hopelessness and when we're hopeless, it's a challenge to dream for the future. We stop making plans. We stop living with purpose. We stop taking righteous risks because we stop believing that God is big enough to redeem our story. But praise God, Naomi got her act together. She started living with a little bit of hope and with it, she created a plan and set it in motion.

I don't see Naomi's suggestion as manipulating God's plan, but rather placing yourself in the position to see God's plan come to pass by actively participating in His story.

God doesn't need our help. However, I believe He loves working with us, not to bring about our own plans, but to bring about His. Paul declares God's desire to co-labor with us in 2 Corinthians 6:1-2, *"Working together with him, then, we appeal to you not to receive the grace of God in vain. For he says, 'In a favorable time I listened to you, and in a day of salvation I have helped you.'"*

Paul reminds us that God is always on time and He gives us the grace to work alongside Him. Could God have brought Boaz and Ruth together some other way? Yes, God can do whatever He pleases. But Naomi's plan was not out of line with the culture of the time or with God's ultimate will.

In this biblical time period, it was not uncommon for servants to sleep at their master's feet, and Ruth had a right to remind Boaz of his position as a Kinsman Redeemer. Regardless of how she approached Boaz, it was God who was ultimately at work. It was their hope that sparked God's action. If it weren't for hope, who knows how long Naomi and Ruth would have sat as characters from the story of their past.

Maybe part of the work we get to do alongside God is simply learning to put our hope in Him. When we place our hope in His mighty hands, it might spark a crazy idea, a righteous risk, that may or may not work. To hope is sometimes an arduous task, especially when we are used to disappointment. But do we still dare to hope? Do we still dare to believe that our hope in God will not be put to shame? Do we still dare to hope that the faithful love of the Lord never ends? Do we still dare to hope when we can't see the harvest?

TABLE TALK

I find it fascinating that God puts such an emphasis on names in the Bible. He even puts emphasis on His own name when speaking with Moses, calling Himself "I AM." Every name has an intentional purpose behind it, and God is no stranger at changing names either. From Abram to Abraham and from Jacob to Israel, God shows us who we are by what He calls us. It seems like whenever a pivotal event takes place, a name is changed, for either better or worse. Look at Paul, who changed his name from Saul after his conversion.

However, Naomi did not change her name for the better in Ruth 1, and I don't think God ever intended for her to call herself Mara. Her name went from meaning "sweet" to meaning "bitter." Through restored hope, she came back to her true name. I love the way Naomi's name never changed throughout the writing in Scripture. She may have given herself a new name, but God never stopped calling her by her true name. What do you speak over yourself in seasons of disappointment? What have you been naming yourself? Who does God say you are?

Righteously Redeemed

Ruth 4, Joshua 2

The last chapter in the story ends with Naomi telling Ruth to "wait." No matter how deeply involved God is in a process, it is still just that- a process. Naomi, Ruth, and even Boaz had to wait to see how events were going to play out with the other Kinsman Redeemer. When the other relative realized that he would acquire Ruth the Moabite, he declined the offer. Maybe he felt caring for Ruth and Naomi was was too big a responsibility. He was concerned about how it would affect his current family's inheritance. Little did he know the role Ruth would play in God's eternal inheritance.

One man's rejection could not stop God's plan. Boaz and Ruth married and gave birth to Obed, King David's grandfather. The book of Ruth ends with this genealogy, which a little further down the line becomes the genealogy of Jesus. This entire story, which can seem a little out of place in the Bible, comes to this unlikely and beautiful conclusion. It all makes sense now. The love story doesn't end with Boaz and Ruth. The redemption doesn't end at Ruth. It keeps going until our Savior is born and redeems us. He is our Kinsman Redeemer!

God will stop at nothing to write our story. He's

involved in the details, and He's been known to seamlessly tie these details together in ways beyond our comprehension. Would a foreign widow, gleaning in Bethlehem's barley fields, ever think that saying "yes" to God meant becoming a part of the family line to the King of all Kings? We never know where God is leading, which is why we must remain in hope and obedience, so we may become threads in His blanket of grace.

TABLE TALK

Read the genealogy of Jesus in Matthew 1. Who is Boaz's mother? What do Ruth and Rahab have in common? Rahab went from prostitute to a biblical heroine who chose the God of Israel over everything (Read Joshua 2). When we place God first in our lives, He redeems the not-so-perfect parts about us. We belong at His table no matter what mistakes we've made or where we've come from. He can use anyone from anywhere to do anything if we simply choose to follow Him.

Is God currently holding first place in your life? Do you feel unworthy of following Him because of where you've come from? Make the bold choice to follow him as Ruth and Rahab did. By doing so, He did extravagant things through them.

day 6

Leftovers Pouring Over

John 6, Matthew 13:53-58

Looking back on the story of Ruth, we know she gleaned or collected the leftover grain from Boaz's field. Boaz even had his servants purposely pull out some of the stalks and leave them for her to glean. Our God is a God of abundance, always ensuring that we not only have what we need but also that we have a blessing that is pouring over. Have our disappointments caused us to doubt that God truly wants abundance for us?

When Jesus fed the 5,000, He asked His disciple Philip where they would get enough food to feed all those people. (He already knew how He was going to make it happen, but He was stretching Philip's faith.) And like any practical person would answer, Philip told Him even if they were to only give away a little bit of food, it would cost them too much money. He didn't answer the question. Jesus asked him, "where?", not "how?"

Where do all miracles come from? Where does our help come from? Where is our hope rooted? I don't know "how" God will answer our prayers or how He will speak to us or how He'll redeem the most broken parts of us, but I know where to look. Philip looked at the situation instead of looking at Jesus and practically said, "There's no way we can feed all these people."

I tend to make circumstances a bigger deal in my head than they really are because I'm so focused on how God's going to work things out. Meanwhile, Jesus tells everybody to sit down in verse 10. Be still. Jesus, Himself, is our abundance, but He delights in answering our impossible prayers and in giving us much more than we deserve. Be still and He will multiply what seems small and make it much...so much, we'll have leftovers.

TABLE TALK

Where are you looking? How is where you are looking causing you to forget who God is? At the beginning of John 6, scripture mentions that many were following Jesus because they saw how He had healed the sick. He was already known for His miracles, signs, and wonders. Feeding thousands of people was not outside of his realm of capabilities. While God is not surprised by our spiritual amnesia, it is important that we don't stay in a place of unbelief. In Matthew 13:58, we learn that Jesus did not perform many miracles in His hometown because of their lack of faith. The people were asking all the wrong questions, instead of asking themselves where to look. Perform a spiritual heart check and ask yourself, "Where am I looking?"

look for Jesus & not all the other things

Averlee's Story

Waiting is hard, especially when you are waiting on something promised by God. I'll never forget the moment I received the promise of a child. I was reading a book on faith. I was all stirred up and heard the Lord say, "Start declaring you are already pregnant." So, my husband and I declared it for two weeks straight. Little did I know, I actually was already pregnant. We were so excited! We didn't expect the promise to be fulfilled so quickly. I manically started planning for our future. What hospital would I deliver the baby at? Did I want a home birth? What do I want to do with the placenta? Pinterest became my best friend. I had boards full of cute maternity clothes, nursery ideas, and essential tips for surviving labor and delivery. I was definitely in baby mode.

One short week later, I became a statistic. I was one of the one in every four women who experience a miscarriage. I was devastated. I knew I had heard from God. Grief hit me hard, but only for one day. Then the most amazing peace covered me like a warm blanket. I could feel God's grace carrying me through, what seemed like, terrain that was impossible to navigate through. I was introduced to new dimensions of God in that season, and discovering the depths with Him was absolutely breathtaking.

A few months later, I found out I was pregnant again. I was excited but hesitant. Unfortunately, this pregnancy came and went more quickly than the first. There were tears, but that peace came back even stronger. The cycle was becoming a little too familiar. That next month, I was pregnant again. I just knew this one was going to be a "sticky bean" because of the third times a charm, right?

Because of my pregnancy history, I was able to schedule weekly doctors' appointments almost right away. Every visit brought the fear of the unknown quickly followed by the excitement of seeing fetal development on the ultrasound screen. Things were looking up until the baby's heart stopped beating. The baby was gone, and they quickly scheduled me for a D&C to "clean everything out."

I was so upset with God. All my faith in His promise drained from my spirit, inch by inch. I was humiliated. How could my body do this to me? How could God do this to me? For the first time, I felt the full weight of grief fall on my shoulders. My doctors told me to stop trying to conceive for at least six months. I knew taking a step back in surrender was necessary, but I wasn't happy about it. My husband and I needed that time to reconnect with God and each other. We had to heal from the emotional wounds that come with losing a child.

As the weeks passed, I became thankful that God allowed me to even experience conception. I was at peace knowing that He was taking care of my little ones in Heaven and that I will meet them up there one day. Which brings me here, coming up on the end of the month waiting period. I have complete assurance that God's promise is going to be fulfilled. When? I'm not sure. In the meantime, I will wait and hold tight to the fact that God has good plans for my husband and me, and our future children.

*Update: Averlee wrote this testimony in August of 2018 and discovered she was pregnant in October. Her baby girl, Monroe, was born in July of 2019.

God of miracles

PARKER HOUSE *rolls*

Serving Size: 12 rolls

INGREDIENTS

1 cup Scolded Milk
¼ cup Sugar
¼ cup Butter
½ teaspoon Salt
1 package of Active Yeast
2 cups sifted All-purpose Flour
¾ teaspoon Baking Powder
¼ teaspoon Baking Soda

DIRECTIONS

1. Pre-heat to 400 degrees.
2. Pour scolded milk over sugar, salt and butter.
3. Stir until butter is melted.
4. Cool it until its lukewarm*; add yeast (stick your finger and if doesn't bite, its good)
5. Stir in flour which has been sifted with baking powder and baking soda; beat well.

6. Let dough rise until doubled in size.**
7. Roll out on floured board, tear golf ball size pieces, roll into little balls.
8. Place in a greased shallow pan.
9. Let rise until doubled in bulk again.
10. Brush with melted butter.
11. Bake in preheated oven for 15 mins.

Tip: When you add milk make sure it's not too hot, it will kill yeast.

**Tip: Cover dough and keep away from drafts while it's rising*

week 5

LOVE FEAST

day 1

Faith & Feasting

Keep trusting in the Lord and do what is right in his eyes. Fix your heart on the promises of God and you will be secure, feasting on His faithfulness. Make God the utmost delight and pleasure of your life, and he will provide for you what you desire most.
Psalms 37:3-4 TPT

God loves a feast. Upon titling this devotional, I had no idea that God really does enjoy a good meal. The correlation between a meal and God's goodness is spun into several stories of promise in the Bible. God always keeps His promises, and He loves to see us celebrate His faithfulness. So much so, that he actually commands it in Leviticus of all books. The last thing I think of when I think Leviticus is a celebration, but Leviticus 23:4 reads, "These are the appointed feasts of the LORD, the holy convocations, which ye shall proclaim at the time appointed for them."

That whole chapter describes these holy feasts that celebrate the faithfulness of God throughout His children's journey. I will dig deeper into a few of these Jewish feasts that are still held to this day, but what I desire for us to grasp is that God delights in our victory as much, if not more, than we do. He directs us to throw a praise party with feasting, drinking, and recounting His marvelous works. It brings Him all the glory when we throw a party in His name, and it causes others to ponder in curiosity. When we feast, it allows us to invite people to the table to join us in marveling at the God who made a way before and will make a way again.

The Greek word for the highest form of love from God is agape. But if you look closely at that definition, the word "love" is paired with the word "feast." What is a feast of love? Could it be that God unabashedly pours out His goodness, mercy, and love on us until we are so full that we are overflowing in abundance? What if we can only feast on His faithfulness if we come and sit at His table?

I love the way the Passion Translation of the Bible translates Psalm 37:3-4. King David praises, "Keep trusting in the Lord and do what is right in his eyes. Fix your heart on the promises of God and you will be secure, feasting on His faithfulness. Make God the utmost delight and pleasure of your life, and he will provide for you what you desire most." God wants us to feast, not starve. When we are hungry, it gives Him the ability to fill us up with more of Himself as we wait for the appointed time for Him to breakthrough for us.

TABLE TALK

Read about the appointed feasts in Leviticus 23. Look up the definition of appointed. What does it mean to you to know that God has already established a specific time for breakthrough in your life before you even feel it? *Just, crazy fai*

Plan your Praise Party! We can and should praise God

in every season, whether waiting or receiving. However, our Heavenly Father delights in seeing us celebrate for His glory. Imagine what you're praying for coming to pass. How will you celebrate? How will you honor God in remembrance for all He's done? Now multiply what you imagine by a hundred because we serve a God of exceedingly and abundantly more. He may not always answer our prayers when or how we expect, but He is a faithful God and I am convinced we will feast on His faithfulness here on earth.

day 2

Feasting on Remembrance

Exodus 12:1-16, Revelation 12:11, Joshua 4:1-9

Passover commemorates the freedom the Israelites received when they were delivered from slavery in Egypt. It is known as the Feast of Salvation. This appointed feast is still celebrated by Jews and Christians around the world, reminding us that the blood of the Lamb still delivers us today from the bondage we find ourselves in.

The Lord had sent plagues on Egypt when Pharaoh wouldn't let the Israelites go and the one that really drove pharaoh's decision to set them free was the plague of the firstborn. This plague killed every firstborn in Egypt, except the ones whose doorposts were marked with the blood of a sacrificial lamb. The Israelites were saved and delivered by the blood of the lamb just like Jesus' blood saves and delivers us from the bondage of sin. The Lord passes over us. He covers us. He rescues us.

The Seder plate is iconic to the Passover meal, not because of what's on it or how it looks, but because of the symbolism behind each item resting on it. The shank bone represents the sacrifice of the lamb on the eve of the exodus. The bitter herbs symbolize the bitterness the Israelites experienced as slaves. Parsley paints the picture of spring and a new beginning. These are just a few of the several symbols that outline this celebration of God's faithfulness. It is the oldest celebrated Jewish festival.

Think about that. People are still celebrating today what God did thousands of years ago. "For the Lord is good and his love endures forever; his faithfulness continues through all generations," proclaims Psalm 100:5. That means that the same God who delivered the Israelites out of Egypt can and will do the same thing for us. So, we feast in remembrance. We break bread in remembrance of Christ's body broken for our sins. We drink in remembrance of the blood He shed. We feast, and we keep feasting in remembrance until our awareness of what God has done becomes greater than our awareness of what we are waiting for Him to do.

TABLE TALK

Reflect on Joshua 4:1-9. Memorial stones were used in Scripture several times to display as a sign of God's faithfulness. Jacob dedicated a stone at Bethel when God gave him a dream (Genesis 28:18). Samuel did the same when the Lord helped the Israelites fight the Philistines (1 Samuel 7:12) and Joshua had appointed twelve men to gather memorial stones after they had successfully crossed the Jordan River into the Promised Land. He commanded the stones to be moved to a place where people could see them.

When our spiritual eyes are fighting to focus, memorial "stones" can be made easily visible to our physical eyes. Create your own memorial stones. Write your own story, poem, or song of remembrance about a time when God made a way for you where there seemed to be no way. You can have several stories. You can put them in individual envelopes with confetti. Fill the envelopes with photos that showcase God's goodness in that specific "Passover" in your life. Then place it somewhere where you can easily recognize it when a cloud fogs your spiritual eyes from recounting God's goodness. Read it. Celebrate it. Remember it.

Feast of Trumpets

1 Corinthians 15:51-57, Leviticus 23:23-25, Joshua 6:1-21

What's a celebration without a little noise? The Feast of Trumpets is often referred to as the Jewish New Year (Rosh Hashanah) and is prophetically linked to the Second Coming of Christ when the last of the seven trumpets will sound and Jesus redeems the earth for His glory.

Trumpets are used throughout the Bible to represent several events. They were used to assemble troops for battle, proclaim a king, warn the people of danger, praise, and declare victory among other things. Whether the reason was good or bad, the sound of a trumpet communicated something important that needed to be said.

One of my favorite mentions of the trumpet is found in Joshua 6. Joshua was leading the Israelites into the Promised Land and the time came to conquer Jericho, but it was a strongly fortified city. The people of Jericho were scared of the Israelites, so the city was shut tight. Joshua 6 literally begins by telling us that there was an impossible wall in front of God's people. But that wasn't the end of the story. God doesn't leave us hanging on one sentence.

The second verse brings forth a different truth. God says, "Look, I have handed Jericho, its kings, and its fighting men over to you" (Joshua 6:2). God also tells Joshua to do something that doesn't make much sense. He commands him and his army to march around the city walls for seven days. The priests were to carry seven trumpets in front of the ark of the covenant (God's presence), and on the seventh day, they were to blow a prolonged blast to signify that the Lord had given them the city. At the sound of the trumpet, on the seventh day, after marching around that wall seven times, the Israelites shouted, and the walls came tumbling down.

The trumpets trembled into the first wave in their ocean of victory. The story doesn't give us perspective on what Joshua or his military thought about marching around this city "aimlessly" for seven days, but I can imagine they probably thought it didn't make much sense. What they thought was aimless was actually strategic. While marching around city walls doesn't look like your typical definition of "being still," I wonder if this battle plan was God's way of commanding His children to do just that. He could stretch their faith and show them that He would fight for them.

These men could have gone in full attack mode, but rather than trying to force themselves into a city that was tightly shut, they surrounded the city. God surrounded the city, too. His presence in the Ark traveled with them every step of the way. The Lord had also already declared the city was theirs before they even experienced the victory. What God declares is final, but we have an active role to play in the story. Joshua was obedient to follow God's command even though it didn't make much sense. Joshua marched anyways, and the troops kept marching even though they were unaware of what the Lord had spoken to Joshua. They didn't know that their last lap was their last lap, just like we don't know when our victory is right around the corner.

Sometimes, the more we feel like we're running in circles, the closer we are to the walls falling down. So, keep your trumpet on hand. Stay the course and hold on to your blasts of praise like you believe the victory is already yours.

TABLE TALK

Let's practice gratitude: What are some things you can blast your trumpet about? How could you view your season of waiting as a strategy God is using to give you the ultimate victory?

My green cord
my new home
He is preparing me for bigger, bigger than I can ever imagine

Reclining At The Table

Mark 4:35-41, Isaiah 58:13-14, Genesis 2:3, Luke 22:14-16

Perhaps the most vital of all feasts is the one that occurs weekly in Jewish culture- Shabbat or the Sabbath. I say the most vital because it's actually commanded in the Ten Commandments, and while Shabbat is observed weekly in traditional Jewish culture, it is also commanded for us to observe as Christians.

Are you good at resting? Even God rested when He was finished creating the world, but it's a foreign concept to us. We love the idea of resting but we live in a culture that is constantly striving, and if we're not striving, we're drowning in our anxious thoughts that keep us from resting. Let me break down this idea with a familiar story found in Scripture since I just mentioned, "drowning."

Remember when Jesus was asleep in the boat during the storm and the disciples were scared to death? They said, "Teacher, don't you care if we drown?" (Mark 4:38), and Jesus told them to chill. He threw out the good ol' "be still." Then He said to them, "Why are you fearful? Do you still have no faith?" (Mark 4:40). Do you still have no faith? Jesus asking this question implies that the disciples had every reason to have faith. They already knew who Jesus was and the miracles He performed, yet it wasn't enough for their weary, anxious minds.

It's easy to forget who God is when we are trembling in fear. We look at the storm and forget who's in the boat with us. Jesus was sleeping on the storm. What would it look like if we rested on the things that we were anxious about? God proclaims that rest is holy, and if we're obedient to get some, He'll see to it that we feast on our inheritance. Even Jesus reclined at the table during the last supper. He knew He was about to be betrayed, yet He reclined.

Let's take that same position at God's table, knowing the ultimate outcome is in His hands. We have something and Someone we can rest in. Our running around trying to solve the puzzles of our lives is making us tired. We're tired of fighting the good fight because we are depending on our own strength to see us through. We cannot sustain ourselves without Him. Jesus, Himself, is our daily meal. We can say, "But you don't know the boat I am in," and while your circumstances may very well be trying to drown you, I can confidently say, "I know Who is in the boat with you. Peace, be still."

TABLE TALK

We talked about the concept of rest in Week 1, Day 4. The reason the subject of "rest" is coming up again is that I believe it's imperative to learn the art of resting in seasons of waiting. Impatience makes us antsy, which tempts us to work towards our dreams and hopes until we can make them happen. When striving ceases, God has room to work. You know the old expression, "If you can't take the heat, get out of the kitchen." We really can't take the heat, nor does God want us to, which is why He calls us to recline at His table instead.

Go back and review what it was you were praying God to work on in Week 1. Declare it out loud or in writing that He is working on those hopes and dreams as you rest. Then rest. Go out with friends, read a good book, go on an adventure, eat a good meal, or just take a really good nap. Whatever rest looks like for you, just get some.

There's More To The Story

Matthew 1:12, 2 Kings 25:27-30, 1 Kings 19:1-9

T he way one story seemingly ends is the way another story begins or continues. The journey is never over until God says it's over and the story is certainly not over if God's promises are not yet fulfilled. The books of 1 and 2 Kings present the line of kings after David in the history of ancient Israel. Corrupt leadership eventually led to the fall of Jerusalem and the exile of the Israelites' into Babylon. Being far from their Promised land, hope seemed lost for David's royal line. They had been unfaithful even after God's many warnings, and because of their unfaithfulness, they were banished from God's promise.

Exile is symbolic of our human condition. This world is not our home and it's full of brokenness, corruption, and idolatry, much like ancient Israel was. We, as God's children, have been experiencing exile ever since Adam and Eve were banished from the Garden. Our disobedience has led us outside of God's best for us. But His grace is greater than our failures. Our disobedience at one tree pointed us towards a Savior who died on another tree.

At the end of 2 Kings, the future of Israel is up in the air. One small and final paragraph is enough to foreshadow that God was not finished yet. Thirty-seven years into Babylonian exile, King Jehoiachin of Judah is released from prison by the evil King of Babylon. We have no explanation as to why, but from that day forward, he dined at the king's table. He was shown favor for the rest of his life.

While 2 Kings doesn't end with a restored Israel, it does birth a fresh hope that it will one day be restored. God had not turned His back on His people, and while Jehoiachin was not perfect by any means, He was still a part of God's eternal plan because of his place in the genealogy of Jesus.

There is always more to the story than what meets the eye. Our mistakes are not greater than God's goodness and mercy that follows us all the days of our lives. What He starts, He intends to bring to completion. We tend to get a little thrown off course when circumstances pull us far from the promises of God, but exile is not eternal. In the thick of it, God sends unlikely provision as He did for Jehoiachin. He ate regularly at the king of Babylon's table. How much more will we receive at our Heavenly Father's table?

TABLE TALK

To understand the idolatry that led the Israelites into Babylon in the first place, it's good to know where the story started. So, let's travel backward to 1 Kings 19 where we see the prophet Elijah use his best efforts to wake up God's people. 1 Kings 19 follows God's miracle at Mount Carmel where he proved to be the true Living God against the false god, Baal. If you don't know the story of God coming by literal fire, then I suggest you read 1 Kings 18, too. The point is, Elijah had witnessed and taken part in many of

God's miracles, yet he ran for his life when he heard the evil queen, Jezebel was out to kill him after God's showdown at Mount Carmel.

He ran into the wilderness, hid under a juniper tree, and asked God to take his life. Why would a man who knew God's faithfulness be suicidal? Even the most gifted prophets experience spiritual amnesia. He went to sleep, but an angel woke him up and gave him food. Then, he slept some more until the angel woke him up a second time. He ate again and then got an assignment from Heaven to go to Mount Horeb, the mountain of God in the Promised Land.

The place of our deepest sadness is not where we are meant to stay. God will send His angels to meet us there, anyway, and they won't tell us to "snap out of it" or make us feel shame for feeling as hopeless as we do. God knows we do better after some sleep and a nice snack. Who are your angels when you're under the juniper tree in the wilderness? Where is God trying to take you next? If we go from glory to glory as scripture says, then we know it's got to be someplace good.

Heaven's Feast

Revelation 19:9, Isaiah 25, 2 Corinthians 4:16-18 (MSG)

The Bible is seamless, echoing God's divine plan for eternity from beginning to end, but even the end isn't really the end. Revelation paints a masterpiece of a day when Jesus returns for His bride, (the church) and the feast that awaits all who call upon His name. This marriage feast between Christ and the church is mentioned not only in Revelation, but also prophesied in the book of Isaiah.

Isaiah 25 celebrates the joy that comes from the glorious return of our Savior, and what better way to celebrate Jesus' return than with a feast? As believers who put our hope in Christ, we really are all waiting on something, something eternal. We're awaiting the promise that Jesus is coming back. As we mentioned yesterday, we are a people living in exile, and this broken world is not our home.

Paul had a steady perspective on our eternity. He didn't give up, no matter what he faced, because he knew what lavish celebration was waiting on the other side. What lavish celebration is on the other side of your waiting, friend? Ultimately, it's an eternity with no more pain and no more tears, but I am convinced that we will see glimpses of heaven on earth on our way there. He'll give us little appetizers along the way to give us just a peek of the feast that awaits us in eternity. Like Paul, we can't lose heart, and we must focus our eyes on what we cannot see. When we spend all of our time looking at what's not going right or what could go wrong, we miss the wonder of the glorious mystery of God. Because He is solely good, we can trust His heart even when we can't see His hand.

As we wait for prayers to be answered, as we wait for promises to be fulfilled, as we wait for Jesus to come back once and for all, our light and momentary troubles are producing for us an eternal glory that we cannot even begin to imagine. We have to get comfortable with the fact that God is comfortable playing the long game. If I am being honest, I'm not quite comfortable with waiting yet, but it is the very nature of how He works. Why would He send the Savior of the world as a child when He could have saved us instantly? I am not sure of His exact reasoning behind why He makes us wait. I guess all of the waiting, hoping and anticipating make for really good storytelling. Or maybe it's because waiting draws us closer to Him, like a child who leans close to a parent at story time, as she anxiously awaits seeing how her bedtime story will end. We lean in as He pours out pieces of His story over us.

TABLE TALK

Read Luke 14:15-24. Jesus tells the Parable of the Banquet to explain that many are invited to His kingdom feast, but poor excuses keep the people from coming. What poor excuses are you using in your relationship with God? Are you too busy? Too tired? Too disappointed? His invitation is open and so are His arms. Use this opportunity to run to Him without restraint. Don't lose heart in the waiting. Come and recline at the table with Him.

day 7

Alexis' Story...As I Sit At His Table

Have you ever experienced the disappointment of ordering something at a restaurant and being told it's not available? The server may politely ask you if you'd be interested in another dish, but you are so set on what you wanted that nothing else on the menu sounds appealing. What if I told you that God has so much more for us than any menu could offer or describe? Here's the catch: you have to let go of all the things you think you want.

I've only recently come to this place of surrender and it is so freeing, I get emotional thinking about it, because for so long, I believed that I couldn't let go. It is a challenge to sit at God's table while simultaneously fighting battles you were never intended to fight. You can't stand and sit at the same time. I used to get incredibly frustrated when people said, "Let go and let God." I am used to having some form of control. When I set my mind to something, I go after it. When I wanted to climb a mountain, I summited one of the highest. When I wanted to run a half-marathon, I trained so I could cross that finish line. When I wanted to travel, I booked a flight. However, there are some dreams in my life that God never intended me to chase and it has taken me a while to realize that His *no's* always point to a greater *yes*.

In the waiting, when we are sitting at God's table, we

may discover that God is preparing something totally different than what we asked for, but that doesn't mean He isn't preparing the very best for you and me. I am not saying that we shouldn't present our requests to God. We should come to Him with everything on our hearts in boldness and confidence. He cares about the desires of our hearts. We just have to end our prayers with, "Your will be done." He knows our desires and our needs more than we do and I am learning to trust that He sees what I don't see.

In the process of writing this devotional, I became so overwhelmed with my own dreams of what I wanted God to do in my life and how I wanted Him to do it. I had unreciprocated feelings for a friend and the rejection ate me alive. Every time I saw him, I asked the Lord, "Why am I not enough? How many times do I have to be rejected?" The anxiety that met me in my waiting room prompted me to book a solo flight to Italy in February of 2019. I spontaneously bought my ticket the day after I watched *Under the Tuscan Sun*. If you are familiar with the story line, then you know that the main character, Frances, receives everything she has ever dreamed of and more. It just comes together in ways she would have never expected.

I embraced every part of that trip. Traveling alone forces you to embrace a place, literally and figuratively. I had nothing but time to wander on the aged cobblestones of Florence and to wander in my spiraling thoughts. It was Valentine's Day and I had signed up for a cooking class with Costanza, the owner of the villa I was staying at. We went out to the garden to pick the ingredients for our meal. With a wise tone and a strong Italian accent, she said to me, "There is beauty in every season." In every season, God can and will use everything together for our good. The grapevines and olive trees may be pruned in the winter, like

I saw in Costanza's garden. But there are still beautiful things growing in the dead of winter, and those olives and grapes will bloom in due season, too.

Whatever dream it is that you are waiting to come to pass, I pray you have the courage to let go of your timeline. I pray you have the courage to let go of the way you think it should be. I pray you let go and surrender all of your hopes of what God might do so that you can grab hold of everything He *will* do.

Friends, I really do dream about being a wife. It may not be a big deal to some, but it has been my dream since I was old enough to have a toy kitchen. God has not opened that door for me, and I've had to watch many friends and acquaintances receive what I so desperately dreamed of while I was still pounding my fist at God. It is the dream that lead me to writing this short devotional and while the season has been arduous at times, I imagine a day where me and my husband are in our very own kitchen. I imagine looking at him with a twinkle in my eye and thinking to myself, "He was so worth waiting for." I hope you have the same experience one day. Whatever you find yourself waiting for, whether it goes the way you planned or not, I pray that God's grace finds you at His table. It's a form of grace that lets us know that God is faithful even when answered prayers look different than we expect. When His grace meets us in our waiting place, *that* is when we *taste and see* that He is good.

Taste and see that the Lord is good. How happy is the man who takes refuge in Him!
Psalm 34:8

SPANISH PICADILLO

savory ground beef in a tomato based sauce

INGREDIENTS

2 lbs of Ground Beef
1 cup of Diced Onions
1 cup of Diced Bell Pepper (green, yellow or red)
½ cup on Chopped Cilantro
4 Recao Leaves
¼ cup of Sliced Olives
2 tbsp. Capers
1 Sazon Envelope (con Culantro y Achiote)
Salt and Pepper to taste
8 oz Tomato Sauce

DIRECTIONS

1. Cook the ground beef with sofrito onions, peppers, cilantro and recao until meat is done.
2. Add salt and pepper while meat is cooking. Add olives, capers and tomato sauce and 2 ounces of water and let cook for about 10-15 minutes on medium or so to cook down any extra liquids. Some cooks add raisins or small cut up potatoes.

3. Drain excess grease and you are ready to serve. Perfect alongside of white rice and sweet plantains. Also, same recipe can be used as stuffing for empanadas.

acknowledgements

A special thank you to Fallen Oak Farms who graciously welcomed me onto their farm so that I could bring my vision for Heaven's Kitchen to life. Your table and your beautiful fallen oak tree are proof that God makes beauty from ashes and His creation echoes His heart. Thank you for being a part of this, Shelley!

A big shout out and thank you to Morgan Harper Nichols for creating the whimsical digital painting on my cover. I am so glad God brought us together at a transitional time in each of our lives. I am so happy to see you blooming. Thank you for encouraging so many of us to stay the course.

Thank you to my family and friends who supported me throughout the time it has taken me to write this devotional. When my faith has been shaken, you remind me to hold on to our God who has always been faithful. Thank you for cheering me on. I love you.

about alexis

In mountains and valleys, my goal is the same: chase the light. Experiencing new adventures, cultures, and landscapes makes my heart come alive. Colors and patterns from God's amazing creation dance in my dreams. I dream big, I dream deep. As a dreamer, sometimes, people don't see what I see, but God has never forsaken me and every dream I've ever had- He has surpassed them all. I am not always the best at trusting God, but one thing I hold on to is that He sets my feet on the peaks and in the valleys. He set a time to reap and a time to sow. He set the moon and sun in the sky so we would never have to walk in the dark. And He's setting things in place for you and me, too. Keep chasing the light.

Check out my website to learn more about me!
https://www.alexisascends.com/

instagram.com/alexismariephoto

pinterest.com/alexismphoto

CPSIA information can be obtained
at www.ICGtesting.com
Printed in the USA
LVHW110207151019
634233LV00001B/73/P

9 781699 220382